MW01095114

Holiness in a Secular Age

Holiness in a Secular Age

THE WITNESS OF
CARDINAL NEWMAN

Fr. Juan R. Vélez

Scepter

Published by Scepter Publishers, Inc.
info@scepterpublishers.org
www.scepterpublishers.org
800-322-8773
New York
All rights reserved.
Text and cover design by Carol S. Cates

Library of Congress Cataloging-in-Publication Data

Names: Vélez, Juan R., author.
Title: Holiness in a secular age : the witness of Cardinal Newman / Fr. Juan R. Vélez,.
Description: New York : Scepter Publishers, 2017. | Includes bibliographical references and index.
Identifiers: LCCN 2017023982 (print) | LCCN 2017025207 (ebook) | ISBN 9781594172823 (ebook) | ISBN 9781594172816 (pbk. : alk. paper)
Subjects: LCSH: Newman, John Henry, 1801-1890. | Catholic Church—Doctrines.
Classification: LCC BX4705.N5 (ebook) | LCC BX4705.N5 V45 2017 (print) | DDC 282.092—dc23
LC record available at https://lccn.loc.gov/2017023982

ISBN pb 978-1-59417-281-6
eBook 978-1-59417-282-3
Printed in the United States of America

Table of Contents

Dedication

For my siblings, Rafael Ignacio, Sergio Enrique, Maria Teresa, and Luz Esther, with whom I share fond and now distant childhood memories of El Pao (Venezuela), Medellin, London and Philadelphia, and with deep gratitude to God and to our parents, Rodrigo and Maria.

Acknowledgments

Expressing recognition and gratitude to all those to whom one is indebted is not an easy task because the list of names is always incomplete. In the first place, I wish to express my gratitude to the editorial and production staff at Scepter Publishers for assisting me in the publication of this volume, in particular to Robert Singerline, Meredith Koopman, Kathleen Hollenbeck, John Powers, and to designer Carol Cates.

This book was written at Northview Study Center, and I wish to acknowledge the friendship and support of those living at the center. My gratitude is also due to Mary Barto for reading and commenting on some of the chapters; to Barbara Wyman, Professor of English and Classics at McNeese University, for providing the preface; to Pat Sharp, who generously edited the original manuscript; and to James Toler for developing and maintaining the website www.cardinaljohnhenrynewman.com.

I would also like to acknowledge my parents, Rodrigo and Maria Vélez. Much credit for this book is indirectly due to them, as they played an important role in my education. To this day, my mother continues to encourage me in my writing projects. Although she reads English, she insists that I translate my book, *Passion for Truth: The Life of John Henry Newman*, into Spanish, a feat that would require much time to do justice to Cardinal Newman's beautiful Victorian English.

I am also indebted to Bishop Javier Echevarria, Prelate of Opus Dei, who ordained me to the priesthood and who has been for me an example of faithfulness and love for God. I am grateful to him for his vibrant transmission of St. Josemaría Escrivá's teachings on holiness and the role of the laity in the Church, which resonate with Blessed Newman's teachings. On December 12, 2016, he was called by God to his eternal reward.

I am also truly grateful for the generous endorsement of my work by the Most Rev. James D. Conley, Bishop of Lincoln, Nebraska, and by Scott Hahn—and to Fr. Robert Matya, pastor of the St. Thomas Aquinas Catholic Church and Newman Center at Lincoln for allowing me to use a photo of the rose window of the beautiful chapel there for the book cover.

Lastly, I wish to recognize Fr. Drew Morgan and the staff of The National Institute for Newman Studies, who have done so much to promote the study of Cardinal Newman through their publications and website (www.newmanreader.org). Fr. John Ford, former editor of the *Newman Studies Journal*, deserves the special gratitude of all who study Newman's life and works.

Foreword

"For they sow the wind, and they shall reap the whirlwind.
The standing grain has no heads, it shall yield no meal."
Hosea 8:7

Cardinal John Henry Newman was a towering figure in nine-teenth century England, one of the great intellects of the time. The nineteenth century, the Victorian Age, was one of many con-tradictions, a century filled with hope but with uncertainty. That uncertainty came from new and destructive modes of thought, the sown wind of Marx, Darwin, Freud, Nietzsche, and others. Many of the challenges Christians face in the current "post mod-ern" age had their beginnings at this time. Cardinal Newman clearly perceived that these modes of thought would lead to con-fusion and endanger souls. In his own time, Newman's writing and his preached sermons, along with his giftedness at being a friend to so many, allowed him to reach every level of society and helped to counter the confusion of the time, as shown clearly throughout this book. To quote from the last chapter of this book:

"Each saint, regardless of the time in which he lives, sheds light and peace around him, making God present to the world. The chapters of this book have been an attempt to show the way that John Henry Newman did this in his own time and continues to do so in ours. This is due in large part to similarities between the nineteenth century and our century, namely, rationalism and ma-terialism as well as growing agnosticism and atheism. Newman addressed these serious ills of society, recognizing with great acuity the roots of the problems and offering the solutions provided by reason and revelation."

Newman's writing and his life continue to impact our current Western society because they speak to the whirlwind that is the result of nineteenth-century winds of destructive thought.

But the meaning of Newman's life can't be expressed only in the context of an academic standpoint. Newman was an intellectual, but he was not only an intellectual. His life was motivated by a much deeper call to holiness, through his love of Christ. Newman attracted others to the faith through his apostolate of friendship more than through debates and argumentation. He drew others along the path to God because he drew them to share in his own personal life, his mind, his heart. As their pastor and mentor, he was also their friend. His motto, "Cor ad cor loquitur" affirms this: "Heart speaks to heart." Newman showed that we evangelize best not by arguing but by friendship. Newman's capacity for deep connection with others, both women and men, is well document-ed in the affectionate letters he wrote to his friends. Newman drew others to Christ through the attraction they felt toward him, their friend and their pastor. Newman's human friendships were integral to his spiritual life, and his friendships brought him closer to God. In this, he is a fine example of how we can best pursue our mission to evangelize. Heart must speak to heart. The human ele-ment is essential if the gift of faith is to take root and bear fruit.

Newman's life and teaching need to be re-presented for the modern world, in order that his thoughts again might reach every level of society, and his heart may continue to speak to our hearts. Fr. Juan Vélez, a pastor and a scholar, a writer and a friend, has done this well. He spent a good portion of the last several years studying and learning about Newman in order to write a biogra-phy: *Passion for Truth: The Life of John Henry Newman.* Fr. Juan was drawn to the person of Newman, Newman's holiness, and Newman's example as a priest and friend to many. To read and condense Newman's thoughts takes a scholar; to interpret New-man's heart and his deep spirituality takes a person who under-stands; to understand the importance of friendship takes one who knows how to be a friend.

My first encounter with Fr. Juan came because of Newman, when, after a chance meeting, and after a just a short time, Fr. Juan learned that I taught at a university. He asked if I was familiar with Newman. When I answered in the affirmative (indeed, Newman played a part in my own conversion to Catholicism, first by his *Idea of the University* and secondly by his writing on the development of doctrine), Fr. Juan asked me to edit the biography he was writing on Newman. And thus began an academic friendship, which later grew into a personal friendship, which now includes the whole family. His example and friendship, like Newman's, encourages others to seek the path of holiness in daily life. Fr. Juan, through courteous and consistent communication and by example, just as did Newman, reminds his many friends to be salt and light. He attracts by affection and friendship. Cardinal Newman's writings fill many books, some which would be inaccessible to most. But the core of his teaching and his school of thought has been clearly explained in a forthright, perceptive way in this book. This book is the perfect way to again bring the holiness and sanctity of Newman to all levels of society, through the sensitive and perceptive words of its author. May the standing grains yield saving fruit. Blessed John Henry, pray for us.

Barbara H. Wyman, M.A., M.F.A.,
Instructor of Classics McNeese State University;
Assistant Director McNeese Honors College
Lake Charles, Louisiana
August 15, 2016

Introduction

Looking at the title of this book, we might wonder: Can more be written about Cardinal Newman? So much has already been published and every year there are more publications about him and his work. Yet, this is the usual case with preeminent men and women in the course of history. Anticipating Newman's future canonization, I wish to offer some of my reflections on this great teacher, addressed especially to the public in general.

Many very good biographies, such as the one by Louis Bouyer and more recently one by Ian Ker, recount the life of John Henry Newman, distinguished English writer, Anglican clergyman and, later, Roman Catholic priest and cardinal. Such biographers offer their account of the life, intellectual talent and religious doctrine of this remarkable nineteenth century English reformer.

However, this work is not a biography—I have written one titled *Passion for Truth: The Life of John Henry Newman*. This work is a monograph on some of Newman's most important contributions to spirituality and theology. I wish to examine some salient points that may be passed over or lost in a biography—for instance: his teaching on holiness, his relationships with the hierarchy or his devotion to Mary. Other contributions by Newman— for example, to literature and interpretation of history, and a renewed study of the Church fathers, among others—will not be addressed because they are more specialized subjects which belong to journals such as the *Newman Studies Journal*.[1] Ker has recently published the book *Newman on Vatican II*, an excellent analysis of Newman's contribution to the council, which deals in more depth

---

[1] For a good treatment of literature and history in Newman see Ian Ker, "John Henry Newman: Analogy, Image and Reality," *Newman Studies Journal*, 12:2 (Fall 2015): 15-32, and Edward Short, "John Henry Newman in the 'Realms of Superstition,'" *Newman Studies Journal*, 12:2 (Fall 2015): 46-74.

on many of the subjects covered in this book. Newman, often referred to as the as "the absent Father" at Vatican II, is called by Ker a "radical conservative." He argues convincingly that Newman would have been a moderate reformer at the council, embracing a hermeneutic of continuity with the past, in contrast to a hermeneutic of discontinuity.[2]

The book begins with a short sketch of his life and continues with chapters that contain biographical information, but which are not meant to be biographical. My purpose is to present the figure of Newman as a man, as a Christian, a priest, a theologian —as a new saint for our times. I wish to draw out what Pope John Paul II saw as the "providential meaning and importance of these events for the Church at large (which) have been seen more clearly in the course of our own century."[3] John Paul II said:

> Newman himself, with almost prophetic vision, was convinced that he was working and suffering for the defence and affirmation of the cause of religion and of the Church not only in his own time but also in the future. His inspiring influence as a great teacher of the faith and as a spiritual guide is being ever more clearly perceived in our own day (. . .)[4]

A few chapters are dedicated to Newman's invaluable teaching about the education of laity and their role in society and in the Church, which preceded the theology of the laity of the twentieth century. One chapter looks at his equally rich teaching on the composition and inspiration of the Scriptures and their relationship to Tradition.

In this volume I also wish to dispel some misunderstandings and erroneous attributions to Newman, commonly made in short articles and public discourses, such as "his" definition of a gentle-

---

[2] Ian Ker, *Newman on Vatican II,* (Oxford: Oxford University Press, 2016, paperback edition), 159.
[3] Letter of John Paul II on the occasion of the Centenary of the Cardinalate of Cardinal John Henry Newman (April 7, 1979), http://www.newmanreader.org/canonization/popes/or21may79.html
[4] *Ibid.*

man, and "his" notions on the authority of conscience or on doctrinal development.

The chapters of this book are invitation to holiness in a secular age in light of the witness of Cardinal Newman. His life and teaching spur us on to greater desires for holiness in everyday life in a world that tries to remove the faith and practice of religion from public life and set up new idols for itself. We should rightly hold Newman as a teacher of the faith and an intercessor in adult faith formation.

His writings are well known to specialists, but now it is time to present them to Catholics at large who would be greatly enriched by his teaching. It is my hope that this book would be used for study and discussion groups as an introduction to Cardinal Newman, for example, at college Newman Centers or in parishes.

Lastly in various chapters I refer to Saint Josemaría Escrivá, founder of Opus Dei, and his successors. In my many years of study of the life of Josemaría Escrivá[5] I have found remarkable similarities in his teachings with those of Blessed John Henry Newman. Despite the differences in their educational and cultural background they both received and developed important insights for the Church in the contemporary world.

In the end, I hope the reader will feel that through these pages he has met Blessed John Henry Newman, and has become his friend, and through this friendship drawn closer to God.

Chicago, April 2, 2016

---

[5] Born in Spain in 1902, only twelve years after the death of Newman, Josemaría Escrivá was ordained a priest in 1925, and founded Opus Dei on October 2, 1928. For a good biography on Escrivá see John Coverdale, *Uncommon Faith: The Early Years of Opus Dei, 1928-1943,* (Princeton: Scepter Publishers, 2002). Both men grew up in societies that became increasingly secularized, agnostic and morally lax, and in which the harmony between faith and science was commonly denied.

Chronology of John Henry Newman

1801	Born in London, February 21.
1808	Enters school at Ealing.
1816	Experiences first religious conversion.
1817	Studies at Trinity College, Oxford.
1822	Is elected Fellow at Oriel College, Oxford.
1824	Is ordained a deacon. Becomes curate of St. Clement's. Death of Mr. Newman.
1825	Is ordained an Anglican clergyman.
1828-43	Becomes Vicar of St. Mary the Virgin.
1831	Resigns tuition at Oxford.
1832-33	Takes trip to the Mediterranean.
1833	Start of the Oxford Movement.
1836	Death of friend R. Hurrell Froude and Mrs. Newman.
1841	Publishes *Tract* 90.
1842	Moves from Oxford to Littlemore.
1845	Is received into the Roman Catholic Church.
1847	Is ordained a Catholic priest in Rome.
1848	Founds English Oratory of St. Philip Neri.
1854-58	Becomes founder and rector of Catholic University of Ireland.
1859	Opens Oratory School in Birmingham.
1864	Publishes *Apologia pro vita sua*.
1877	Is elected first honorary fellow at Trinity College.
1879	Is created cardinal by Pope Leo XIII.
1889	Celebrates last Mass, on Christmas Day.
1890	Dies in Birmingham, August 11.

Abbreviations

One

LIFE OF JOHN HENRY NEWMAN: BIOGRAPHICAL SKETCH

John Henry Newman (1801-1890) was one of the great Englishmen of the nineteenth century; perhaps one could call him a Victorian, yet he was very different from other famous Victorians such as Charles Dickens, George Elliot, or William Gladstone. He was an Anglican convert to Catholicism, a Catholic priest, and later a cardinal. Like many of the celebrated Victorians, he was a man of letters, a prolific writer, and an influential figure in public life.[1]

His extensive intellectual and literary legacy makes of him an attractive figure, one often quoted, and more often misquoted—a thinker whose endorsement is sought by Catholic writers in doctrinal and moral matters. Liberals and religious conservatives seek him as standard-bearer for their positions. But Newman was neither; he should instead be considered orthodox, indebted as he was to the doctrinal principle in religion. He was controversial because he voiced his beliefs in difficult subjects of the day, relying on the logical consequences of accepted Christian premises.

Born in London on Old Broad Street, where the London Stock Exchange stands today, he was the oldest of six children in the family of John Newman and Jemima née Fourdrinier. Mr. Newman, son of a Cambridge grocer, was a banker. His wife, daughter of a wealthy papermaker, was descended from French Huguenots. The family was Low Church Anglican, and in addition to morn-

---

[1] For a good overview of his writings see John T. Ford, "John Henry Newman: A Short Introduction to his Writings," *Newman Studies Journal*, 12:2 (Fall 2015): 33-44.

ing and evening prayers, they attended Sunday service in church. Newman was baptized less than two months after his birth, and his grandmother Elizabeth Good and aunt Elizabeth Newman read to him the Sacred Scriptures from an early age.

The family enjoyed material comfort and, unlike most children of the period, Newman attended a boarding grammar school in Ealing, just outside London. There he excelled in his studies, including Latin, and won competitions in writing. He also learned to play the violin, a pastime that he would enjoy for the rest of his life.

In March 1816, Mr. Newman's bank failed and the family suffered financial difficulty. That summer, young Newman remained at school and, while convalescing from an illness, came under the strong religious influence of Walter Mayers, a Calvinist clergyman. During this time he experienced what he would later call his first conversion: a conscious awareness of God's existence and providence in his life, and of the importance of religious doctrine.

The following year, Mr. Newman took his son to Oxford and enrolled him at Trinity College where, after a difficult start because of his strict religious beliefs and youth, the young man did well. In 1818, he won a scholarship at Trinity, but in 1820, out of overexertion in study and fear of failure, he did not obtain the desired honors in his final undergraduate examinations. For a short while he considered—at his father's promptings—a career in law, but in 1822, he finally decided to become a clergyman instead and was elected a fellow at Oriel College. At that time, Oriel was one of the most prestigious colleges at Oxford. As a fellow, he lived and studied in the company of other bright men who helped him to reason better, overcoming simple fundamentalist ideas in religion.

Some years later, Newman became a tutor at Oriel where, with Provost Edward Hawkins and other tutors, he had undergraduates under his care. This would prove a great experience for him but would also lead to a significant collision with the provost. In keeping with an ancient Oxford tradition, practically lost by the time Newman was at Oxford, he thought that a tutor should care not only for the intellectual but also for the moral and religious lives of his students. In this effort, he engaged the help of two younger tutors, Isaac Wilberforce, a later Catholic convert and second son of the abolitionist, William Wilberforce and Richard Hurrell Froude, and together they attempted to reform Oriel's educational system. After a few years of individual success with students, however, the provost deprived the reformers of future students. Edged out of Oriel, Newman decided to accompany his friend Froude, who was suffering from pulmonary tuberculosis at the time, and Archdeacon Froude, the latter's father, on a long trip to the Mediterranean.

Their visits to some Greek islands and later to Rome, with its churches and ancient monuments, made a particularly memorable impression on Newman. The young Anglican clergyman experienced the contrast of the remains of ancient civilizations and early Christianity. In long and detailed letters to his family members and friends, he expressed the sentiments he felt regarding the greatness of ancient Greece and Rome, all the while aware of their pagan customs, and walked over the sites hallowed by the first Christians.

It was, however, in Sicily, after separating from the Froudes, where he had a powerful conversion experience. After a very brief visit to Syracuse, he fell sick, most likely due to typhoid fever, from which he almost died. For a number of weeks, while convalescing in the interior of the island and at Palermo, he had the clear conviction that he was to be spared for some divine purpose. It was at sea on his return trip to England that he penned the now-famous poem *Pillar of the Cloud*, asking God to lead him and trusting in his all-powerful providence:

LEAD, Kindly Light, amid the encircling gloom
   Lead Thou me on!
The night is dark, and I am far from home—
   Lead Thou me on!

Keep Thou my feet; I do not ask to see
The distant scene—one step enough for me.[2]

Within a week of returning to Oxford, Newman met with John Keble, Froude, Hugh James Rose, and a few others, who agreed to launch a spiritual renewal of the Anglican Church. It was an informal plan, with deep doctrinal roots, which sought to strengthen the moral authority of the bishops. It consisted in the publication and distribution of tracts as well as sermons, most notably those of Newman delivered at St. Mary's University Church before expectant congregations of students and professors. The young Oxford clergyman cast a spell on his audience with a deep draught of biblical truths, awakening his listeners to an exacting call to holiness in everyday life and greater faithfulness to the Church's liturgy and norms.

The influential Oxford Movement had begun, and soon Edward B. Pusey, a Hebrew scholar, as well as other younger and deeply committed men joined its ranks. Dean Church, Edward Manning, and other important Anglicans would later partake in the movement. Almost from the start, it met resistance from the "high-and-dry" high Anglican establishment as well as from the Low Church Anglicans of the Calvinist cast. Various developments in ecclesiastical life made the claims of the movement more pressing and controversial. The breaking point came with Newman's publication of *Tract* 90 in which. for the sake of keeping men from going over to Rome, he argued that the Thirty-Nine Articles of the Anglican Church were compatible with Catholic teaching. In fact, many Anglicans regarded themselves as within the larger Catholic body. Newman's enemies denounced the tract to a bishop, and one bishop after another added his condemnation. This was a painful time for Newman, who regarded himself Anglican in all respects and who only sought the doctrinal and spiritual strengthening of the Church.

---

[2] John Henry Newman, "The Pillar of the Cloud," in *Verses on Various Occasions* [June 16, 1833], London: Longmans, Green, and Co., 1903), 156.

His days as an Anglican were, however, numbered; he felt in conscience that he must cease his duties as a clergyman. He moved permanently to the village of Littlemore, just outside Oxford, where he spent some years praying and studying with men younger than he who sought out his company. Gradually they individually came to the moral conviction that they should be received into the Roman Catholic Church. On the evening of October 8, 1845, Newman began his confession before Italian Passionist Fr. Dominic Barberi, a visiting missionary, who was overcome with emotion upon seeing the distinguished Newman coming to him for this purpose. On the morrow, Newman and a few of his companions recited the Creed and were admitted into communion with the Church of Rome.

It had been a long and arduous process of discernment, with careful examination of claims and intentions, until the final, irrevocable decision. Newman was forty-four years old, an established writer, a tutor at Oxford, and an Anglican clergyman. He was venturing on faith, as he had said in an earlier sermon. He had taken a momentous step because he felt that, given the lights that he had received, he—not others—must take this step to save his soul. He had reached a safe port after a difficult journey and would live another forty-five years as a Roman Catholic priest and cardinal. Although he would suffer a great deal as a Catholic due to misunderstandings by Anglicans and Catholics alike, he never regretted his decision.

Thus, Newman became Catholic after many years of prayer and study of Christian doctrine and history. During the immediate four years before his reception, he labored over the notion of a true and false development in Christian doctrine: to ascertain whether in reality the Roman Catholic Church was a corruption or a true development from early Christianity. The result of his study was an important book, *An Essay on the Development of Christian Doctrine*, which in fact remained incomplete when he put his pen down as an Anglican on the first week of October 1845.

After a short period as a Roman Catholic, at the suggestion of Bishop Nicholas Wiseman, Apostolic Vicar to the Midland District of England, Newman and a few fellow converts traveled to Rome where they studied for ordination to the priesthood at the College of Propaganda Fidei. On Trinity Sunday, May 29, 1847, Newman and Ambrose St. John were ordained, and, shortly afterward, they returned to England to begin, as was their desire and the wish of Pope Pius IX, the English Oratory of St. Philip Neri. The Oratory was established in Birmingham and had under its care a parish that served poor Irish immigrants. Shortly after its establishment, Frederick William Faber, a young convert and talented writer, prevailed on Newman to join him with a group of converts. Almost immediately, Faber's excessive zeal to bring about conversions to the Catholic faith and preference for Italian expressions of piety created difficulties at Birmingham, and Newman was obliged to open the Brompton Oratory in London for Faber and some of his followers.

Faber became a close friend of Wiseman, who was named Archbishop of Westminster, the Catholic diocese of London. Moved by different ideas about the purpose of the Oratory, and out of jealousy, Faber raised suspicions concerning Newman in the mind of Wiseman, who blocked a number of important projects that Newman wished to pursue. One of these was a new English translation of the Bible entrusted to him by the First English Synod of Bishops following the restoration of the English hierarchy.

After the death of Wiseman and Faber, two other influential men—Edward Manning, Wiseman's successor, and Msgr. James Talbot, his agent in Rome—caused comparable suffering to Newman in Rome. The latter made him suspicious in the eyes of Propaganda Fidei, and they blocked Newman's desire to open an oratory at Oxford. In fact, toward the end of Newman's life, they almost succeeded in blocking his reception of the cardinalate granted him by Leo XIII.

One of Newman's greatest achievements was the formulation of fundamental ideas about the nature of a university education and the actual establishment of the Catholic University of Ireland in 1854. Although the university did not continue for a variety of reasons mostly out of Newman's control, its founding gave him the occasion to compose his masterful *Idea of a University* which, together with his *Sketches on University Education* and various discourses to schools at the university, as well as the day-in and day-out running of the university, has provided a lasting contribution to Catholic liberal arts education.

As a Roman Catholic, Newman wrote many memorable works. The one that most rapidly gained respect for him, both from Catholics and Anglicans, was his *Apologia pro vita sua*, an intellectual biography of the development of his religious beliefs. After the apparent earlier failure and many contradictions in Dublin, the success of the *Apologia* gave Newman new impetus in his writings and dealings with others. Another one of Newman's major intellectual contributions was *Grammar of Assent*, the result of more than twenty years of considering the subject of the act of faith and the certitude reached by the believer.

Permanently back in Birmingham after resigning as rector from the Catholic University of Dublin, he resumed his pastoral work and supervision of the Oratory. A few years later he engaged in one last educational work: the establishment of a Catholic Eton: a boarding school with the prestige of English public schools like Eton, and with the Catholic ethos and sacramental life. To the end of his long life he would devote his efforts to the formation of students and the many faceted difficulties of the administration of a school.

In 1877, Newman was elected the first honorary fellow at Trinity College, Oxford. When he visited for the first time after his departure in 1844, he was kindly welcomed. Then in 1879, after returning from Rome with the cardinal's hat, he was honored by many throughout England. He was a champion returning from receiving a great prize—a tribute to him and to the English people.

Newman was an old and wise man: humble, gentle, and kind. He prayed, offered the Sacrifice of the Mass, and served his community as much as he could even as his strength withered away year by year. His last years were peaceful; he maintained his intellectual sharpness, but his body could not respond to the usual demands of life and he suffered prolonged colds. In the end, his correspondence—by then dictated to his faithful secretary Fr. William Neville—diminished considerably both in number and length. He had run the race and completed his work on earth. After a relatively short respiratory infection, he died on the morning of August 11, 1890, to be mourned immediately by all his countrymen. His remains were buried on the grounds of Rednal, the Oratory country house in Edgbaston just outside Birmingham.[3]

During his life, Newman was recognized for his intellectual brilliancy and literary composition. He was also admired for his charity and piety. Today, after having been declared *beatus* (blessed) by Pope Benedict XVI on September 20, 2010, he is venerated by Catholics.

[3] In 2008, the exhumation of his grave did not reveal any physical remains. His corpse had completely decomposed because he was buried in a wooden coffin, and the gravesite at Rednal was damp.

Two

ON FRIENDSHIP

Cicero's classic definition of friendship was no doubt well known to Newman, who delighted in the Roman orator's rhetoric. Cicero wrote:

> For friendship is nothing else than an accord in all things, human and divine, conjoined with mutual goodwill and affection, and I am inclined to think that, with the exception of wisdom, no better thing has been given to man by the immortal gods.[1]

The Oxford don's dealings with friends were indeed characterized by "mutual good will and affection," as can be gleaned from the mention of his relationships with them.

Perhaps Newman's first friend and one of his closest was William Bowden, with whom he studied at Trinity College, Oxford; they had met the first day of Newman's arrival at Oxford. Bowden was one year his senior, but they shared the same birthday. After graduating, Bowden took a position in the postal service in London, where Newman would visit him and his family. The visits increased when Newman learned Bowden was suffering a serious illness. Newman thought that his friend's death would be like severing ties with Oxford because everything associated with the university had to do with his friend. After Bowden's premature death, Newman remained a close friend with his wife and children, rendering them many services.

---

[1] Cicero, *Laelius de Amicitia (on Friendship)*, 6. Website: http://penelope.uchicago.edu/Thayer/E/Roman/Texts/Cicero/Laelius_de_Amicitia/text*.html.

Richard Hurrell Froude was another very close friend of Newman. They had many long and deep conversations about religion,
history, and politics. Froude was an Anglo-Catholic who did not
refrain from lively debates with Newman, then an Anglican with
Evangelical leanings, while they were both tutors at Oriel College.
Their friendship exemplifies Newman's openness to learn from his
friends. He accompanied Froude, who was ill with tuberculosis,
on a long Mediterranean voyage, hoping the climate would improve his friend's health. Froude did not live long after the trip,
and his early death caused Newman much pain.

At Oxford, Newman also became very close friends with John
Keble and Edward B. Pusey, both accomplished in their teaching,
Keble in poetry and Pusey in Hebrew. They were devout Christians and high Anglicans. As with Bowden and Froude, Newman
also became good friends with their families. Their friendships
grew and solidified as they invested themselves wholeheartedly in
a common cause: the spiritual, doctrinal and liturgical renewal of
the Anglican Church. Keble, although older than Newman,
sought Newman's spiritual guidance in sundry matters. And Pusey
found solace in Newman's affection during the illness and death
of various family members.

As a tutor, Newman gave of himself to his students. He was
more than a teacher; he was like a father and a friend. He gave
them example and inspired them. They went together on walks or
horseback rides. During the summers he invited some to stay with
him at country parishes, guiding their reading for various subjects
while he took on pastoral duties for friends. One of his best students, Frederick Rogers, excelled under Newman's care, and afterward always remembered his teacher. Another student, Tom Mozley, as well as his brother John, married Newman's sisters, Harriet
and Jemima, respectively.

When Newman retired into lay communion in the Anglican
Church and moved to Littlemore, various young men were drawn
to join him there. His association with them took on deep bonds
of spiritual friendship. Most of these men converted along with

Newman, or a few days before him, and later went with him to Rome, where he became the first priest for the Oratory in England. In letters to two of these, Ambrose St. John and John Dalgairns, he addressed them with the affectionate Latin term "charissime" (sic) for "dearest." He would do the same for Henry Wilberforce, another Oxford friend, and sign with closures such as "Charissime, you are ever in my thoughts," and to other close friends with "Ever yours affectionately," and in typical manner with his initials: "J.H.N."

What, then, of the suggestion that Newman was withdrawn, timid, and overly sensitive? He was certainly studious and hard-working, but not withdrawn. He was reserved rather than timid or lacking in self-confidence. Like St. Augustine, Newman had a very good knowledge of his own sentiments, fears, desires, and ambitions, and was a good judge of character. Thus he felt more keenly the expressions of gratitude or ingratitude, sincerity or insincerity of others, producing at times disquiet or sadness.

Loyalty was another characteristic of Newman's friendships. After the publication of the *Apologia pro vita sua* in 1864, Newman was able to rekindle his friendship with a number of close Anglican friends from his time in the Oxford Movement. The encounters with Keble and Pusey were not easy because many years had passed since their last meeting, and strong memories of a long-ago past rose before them. And worthy of note, Frederic Rogers, later Lord Blachford, as well as William Church, William Copeland, and Lord Coleridge, gave Newman the gift of a carriage when he returned to England as a cardinal.

This rekindling of old friendships is also a tribute to these men's charity and loyalty. They had been separated due to painful religious differences and social circumstances, but they had maintained their affection and goodwill. They were friends.

Newman was able to identify the talents of his friends and to help them develop these gifts, especially the intellectual ones. Working on various projects meant new friendships. Just as he had become a friend to many through the Oxford Movement, once a Roman Catholic, he made good friends with others working with them in various educational projects; thus, the friendship with Edward Bellasis, James Hope-Scott, John Hungerford Pollen, and others. These men had great admiration and refinement in their dealings with Newman, who knew how to respond with gratitude for their confidence in him as well as solicitude for their needs.

As the years went by, Newman lived through the passing away of many friends. Each death meant the end of an intimate association. In 1872, he pronounced the funeral sermon at the deaths of James Hope-Scott and William Henry Wilberforce. Their friendships, however, lived on, not only through fond memories but also in the communion of the saints—the bond of love and prayer that is not sundered by distance or death. On the walls of his small personal chapel hung many paintings and photos of his patron saints and deceased friends. He also kept the dates of their feast days or death anniversaries in a calendar to remember them in a special manner at Mass.

His friendship naturally extended to his brothers at the Birmingham Oratory, including Fr. Joseph Gordon, who died an early death; Fr. Ambrose St. John, his closest friend once he became a Roman Catholic; and Fr. Henry Ignatius Ryder, his successor as head of the Oratory. St. John, of a different temperament and talents—he was a Greek scholar and knowledgeable in German and other modern languages—entered into Newman's ideas and sentiments, fully appreciating his genius, and loyally collaborating with him.

When Ambrose St. John died, Fr. William Neville, a convert and priest of the Oratory, took his place as Newman's helper and secretary in his old age. Neville loved Newman as a father and cared for him to the day of his death on August 11, 1890. As a sign of his trust, Newman had made Fr. Neville executor of his will. In the preface of Newman's posthumous *Meditations and Devotions*, a beautiful collection of prayers composed by Newman and translations from the breviary, Neville wrote in the names of a number of cardinals and archbishops whose names Newman desired to have associated in some way with him on account of their friendship and service. At the end of the list Neville wrote: "One name there is to mention—and it belongs to America, where though our Cardinal had so many friends, one was pre-eminently such—that of Bishop James O'Connor, Bishop of Omaha, whose unaffected kindness was most grateful to our Cardinal, lasting as it did through all but the whole of his Catholic lifetime." They had first become friends while studying at Propaganda Fidei in Rome.

Maintaining the natural bounds of prudence throughout his life, Newman also developed friendships with women. As scholar Edward Short has observed, he wrote to his mother and sisters and some female friends with "extraordinary candor and depth."[2] Among these were Mrs. William Bowden and her daughter Marianne; family friends Maria Giberne, Elizabeth (Isy) Froude and Emily Bowles; Ms. Mary Holmes, a governess; authors Lady Chatterton and Lady Georgiana Fullerton; and Anne Mozley, his sister-in-law. He helped them live out their respective vocations in marriage or religious life, and gave them encouragement in their charitable and literary works. Drawing on Newman's correspondence with them, Short concludes:

> In the wonderful correspondence between Newman and his women friends—which if culled from the letters as a whole would capture the very essence of the man—we can see what a Christ-like affection Newman felt for those good, devoted, brave women, who meant so much to the Church, in its uncertain Second Spring.[3]

Newman was an excellent correspondent. Through the custom of letter writing he informed friends of his ideas and activities and inquired about their lives. Understandably for a man of letters like

[2] See Edward Short, *Newman and his Contemporaries*, (New York: T & T Clark, 2011), 178.
[3] Short, 212.

he was, he once wrote a friend explaining how he liked the early
saints more than the medieval saints because, from their extant
letters which capture their way of being:

> . . . letters always have the charm of reality. I have before now
> given this as the reason why I like the early Fathers more than
> the Medieval Saints viz: because we have the letters of the
> former. I seem to know. St. Chrysostom or St. Jerome in a
> way in which I never can know St. Thomas Aquinas—and St.
> Thomas of Canterbury (himself medieval) on account of his
> letters as I never can know St. Pius Vth (sic).[4]

For his part, Newman left a similar record of his personality. From
his numerous letters to family and friends, it is easy to see his good
humor and very sharp wit; drawing on his keen capacity for obser-
vation and mastery of language, he was able to capture in words
his flaws and those of others, to make light of them.

His letters are full of humorous—sometimes even hilarious—
descriptions, such as his arrival by ship at Naples and the pick-
pockets of the city, or how its post office ate up his mail. Another
example was his account of the visit of someone who, with the
enthusiasm of a recent convert, tried to convert him. Newman
wrote a friend: "I have kept my gun loaded and cocked, intending
to discharge it upon him, if he made a second attempt, but he has
kept his peace."[5]

At the end of his life, when created a cardinal in 1878, he chose
for his episcopal motto the words "Cor ad cor loquitur" (heart
speaks to heart), taken from a letter of St. Francis de Sales, the
seventeenth-century French bishop. That, in effect, is what
friendship is: an ongoing heart-to-heart conversation between
persons, with Jesus' friendship as the paradigm. The letter may
have been one from St. Francis to St. Jane de Chantal in which he

[4] John Henry Newman to Mrs. Sconce, (October 15, 1865), *The Letters and Diaries of John Henry Newman*, Vol. 22, ed. Charles Stephen Dessain et al (Oxford and London: 1961-), 73-74. 73. From here on *LD*.
[5] JHN to John Dobree Dalgairns, (May 9, 1845), *LD, Vol. 10*, 651-653; 652.

said that he wished to write her with complete freedom, not holding back any thoughts and affections: "I want to speak to you heart to heart."[6] De Sales told Chantal, who already had a spiritual director, not to worry about receiving advice from someone else—provided her spiritual father had first place:

> I am all yours; give no more thought to the role or to the rank I hold in being yours. God has given me to you; so consider me as yours in Him, and call me whatever you like; it makes no difference.[7]

Newman, too, expressed his thoughts and affection freely in letters to his friends. He and the holy bishop were no doubt different, yet they had in common—also with Paschal, whom Newman cited a number of times—a deep understanding of the role of the heart in loving God and others. With his friends, Newman was not as copious in the expression of feelings as De Sales, yet he conveyed to them his warmth, trust, and affection.

In addition to affection and loyalty, there were other aspects of friendship, such as sincerity, practiced by Newman. With friends he shared openly his religious and political views as well as his sentiments, doubts, and worries. When necessary, this same sincerity led him to point out mistakes and errors to them and to others.

Above all, for Newman, friendship consisted in Christian charity, a generous selfless service of others for love of God. He lived this service in his relationship with his siblings and later with his friends and parishioners at Oxford. The parishioners would recall his visits to the sick of the parish. Newman visited and comforted his friends when they were ill or had lost a loved one. Moved by charity, he spent himself helping his students advance in their studies and grow in character. He also gave people recommenda-

---

[6] Francis de Sales, Letter of St. Francis de Sales to St. Jane de Chantal, June 24, 1604, in *Francis de Sales, Jane de Chantal: Letters of Spiritual Direction*, ed. Péronne Marie Thibert, V. H. M., Wendy M. Wright, and Joseph Power, O. S. F. S. (Mahwah, N.J.: Paulist Press, 1988), 126.

[7] *de Sales*, 127.

tions for employment and helped those he could to find positions.

With Newman, human friendships led in a natural way to discussions and correspondence on spiritual matters. He learned from his close friends such as Froude, Bowden, Keble, and Pusey. Together they grew spiritually even when their religious paths diverged. He asked God to help his friends through his example—which explains how, when he became Roman Catholic, many friends and acquaintances were aided by him. He prayed to God:

> Make me preach Thee without preaching—not by words, but by my example and by the catching force, the sympathetic influence, of what I do—by my visible resemblance to Thy saints, and the evident fulness of the love which my heart bears to Thee.[8]

As with De Sales, Newman offered spiritual direction to many people through written correspondence. In Newman's case, many of his correspondents had been students with him or under him at Oxford, and others were connected to him through family relations to his friends. Over time, friendships arose between Newman and these individuals, and within these friendships, relationships of spiritual direction developed. In other instances, friendships arose with people after they sought Newman out to consult him on religious or spiritual matters.

Many other lessons could be learned from a study of friendship in Newman, perhaps drawing from his ample correspondence with friends since he did not write, to my knowledge, an essay on friendship per se. And were it not that there are other subjects on which he wrote and made significant contributions to theology, one day he could well be remembered for this.

Pope Pius XII predicted that Newman would eventually be declared a Doctor of the Church.[9] Recently, Oratorian Father Drew

---

[8] John Henry Newman, *Meditations and Devotions of the Late Cardinal Newman*, ed. William Neville (London: Longmans, Green, and Co, 1907), 365. From here on *M.D.*
[9] Vincent Ferrer Blehl, S. J., *The White Stone: The Spiritual Theology of John Henry Newman* (Petersham, Mass.: St. Bede's Publications, 1993), 187.

Morgan explained why a saint is given the title "Doctor of the Church" and why there is ample reason to expect that this will be most apropos in Newman's case.[10] Each doctor is given a title that makes reference to some special trait or doctrine. One could thus imagine that, if after his future canonization Newman were declared a Doctor of the Church, one of his possible titles would be *doctor amicitiae* (Doctor of Friendship).

---

[10] See Drew Morgan, "John Henry Newman—Doctor of Conscience: Doctor of the Church?" *Newman Studies Journal*, 4: no. 1 (Spring 2007), 5-23.

Three

HOLINESS AND CHRISTIAN LIFE

From an early age, Newman learned Christian piety at his home, especially with his grandmother Elizabeth Good and aunt Elizabeth Newman. At the age of 14, however, he entertained religious doubts and enjoyed reading objections to Christianity by writers like Thomas Paine, David Hume, and Voltaire.[1] Of these objections he even remarked, "How dreadful, but how plausible."[2] In this frame of mind he wanted to be virtuous but not religious. Then the following year, at the boarding school in Ealing, he had a spiritual conversion and was inspired to see Christian life in terms of religious truths (doctrine) and holiness. Walter Mayers, the Calvinist clergyman who ran the school, taught the young man to live a devout Christian life.

Newman would later write in his autobiography:

> When I was fifteen (in the autumn of 1816), a great change of thought took place in me. I fell under the influences of a definite Creed, and received into my intellect impressions of dogma, which, through God's mercy, have never been effaced or obscured. Above and beyond the conversations and sermons of the excellent man, long dead, the Rev. Walter Mayers, of Pembroke College, Oxford, who was the human means of this

---

[1] Newman recalls having read Paine's tracts with objections against the Old Testament, some of Hume's essays—perhaps the one on miracles—and some French verses by Voltaire denying the soul's immortality. See John Henry Newman, *Apologia pro vita sua*, [1865] (London: Longmans, Green, and Co., 1908), 3. From here on Apo.

[2] *Apo.*, 3.

beginning of divine faith in me, was the effect of the books which he put into my hands, all of the school of Calvin.[3]

The young man read *The Force of Truth*, the autobiography of Thomas Scott, a famous Evangelical and biblical commentator, in which the author described his spiritual journey from Unitarianism to belief in the Holy Trinity.[4] He learned and embraced the doctrine on the Incarnation and Redemption, and the indwelling of the Holy Spirit, emphasized by Scott. Newman was impressed by two of Scott's maxims: "holiness rather than peace," and "growth, the only evidence of life." When he went to Trinity College, Oxford, a few years later he began to put this maxim into practice, resisting the heavy drinking of his college peers.

At a young age, inspired by Scott's Essays and the work of Jones of Nayland,[5] he began to study the content of the Scriptures and the Creed. He tried to find passages in Scripture to substantiate the articles of the Athanasian Creed. Thus early on in life, Newman's religious beliefs were centered on the Christian doctrine on the Holy Trinity. God revealed himself in Christ as Three Divine Persons, and, therefore, to know God means to seek the knowledge of the Trinity rather than some abstract creative power in the universe.

Religious doctrine founded on Sacred Scripture would be the firm basis for all of Newman's spiritual life. Many years later, in the *Grammar of Assent* (1870), his last major work, he explained that belief in God is a real assent instead of a notional one. This belief is based on the voice of a person's moral conscience. He felt that already at a young age, a child is able to discern right from

---

[3] *Apo.*, 4.

[4] Thomas Scott (1747-1821) had only converted to a Trinitarian creed a few years before Newman read his writings. Newman was deeply impressed by him and in the *Apologia* writes of him as "the writer who made a deeper impression on my mind than any other, and to whom (humanly speaking) I almost owe my soul." See *Apo.*, 5.

[5] William Jones (1726-1800), a graduate of Oxford University, was a high Church man and curate of Nayland in Suffolk. Newman probably read his tract *The Catholic Doctrine of a Trinity*.

wrong and that when he does wrong, there is One that he is offending whom he does not see; and that this Lawgiver and Judge not only enjoins and enforces what is right or wrong but kindles love in the child toward himself.[6]

Newman's sermons are imbued with a Trinitarian dimension, which is to say they are close to Jesus' revelation in the Gospels of the Father and the Holy Spirit. Throughout the sermons there are references to the three divine Persons. Those who heard him—and later his readers—were drawn into the mystery of the God who reveals his inner life to man. Newman believed that the God who reigns in heaven surrounded by angels is all-holy; he is a consuming fire. He brought his audience before this majestic revelation of God, before his holiness.

As has been noted by Fr. Vincent Ferrer Blehl, Newman rediscovered under the influence of the Eastern Fathers of the Church the doctrine of the indwelling of the Holy Spirit and his sanctifying action on the soul.[7] Through Baptism the Holy Spirit, sent by the Father and the Son, unites the Christian to Christ and to his mystical body. In this way Newman anticipated the teaching on the role of the Holy Spirit in the life of the baptized reiterated in the Second Vatican Council.

Newman further asserted that the Christian must acknowledge his imperfection and sinfulness before God, aspiring to be perfect as his Father in heaven is perfect. It is telling that he placed a sermon on holiness as the first one for the volumes of the Parochial and Plain Sermons. This is the importance that he attached to holiness as the foundation for a religious life. The sermon was titled "Holiness Necessary for Future Blessedness," in which he would answer the question:

> Why is it that holiness is a necessary qualification for our being received into heaven? why is it that the Bible enjoins upon us so strictly to love, fear, and obey God, to be just, honest,

---

[6] John Henry Newman, *An Essay in Aid of a Grammar of Assent*, [1870], (London: Longmans, Green, and Co., 1903), 114. From here on GA.

[7] Blehl, 186.

meek, pure in heart, forgiving, heavenly-minded, self-deny-
ing, humble, and resigned? Man is confessedly weak and cor-
rupt; *why* then is he enjoined to be so religious, so unearthly?
why is he required (in the strong language of Scripture) to
become 'a new creature'?[8]

Newman readily noted that God could have saved us in other
ways and then went on to explain his conclusion: "I answer as follows: That, even supposing a man of unholy life were suffered to
enter heaven, *he would not be happy there*; so that it would be no
mercy to permit him to enter." On earth everyone can seek his
own pleasures, but in heaven he must do God's pleasure, he said.
Newman then compared heaven to a church where the object of
attention is God and the activity is his praise and thanksgiving. A
non-religious person finds no satisfaction in a church and thus
would not find it either in heaven: "If then a man without religion
(supposing it possible) were admitted into heaven, doubtless he
would sustain a great disappointment."[9]

Here, as in many other sermons, Newman presented worship as
an essential part of holiness. A much later sermon, for instance, is
titled "Worship, a Preparation for Christ's Judgment." Prayer
molds the heart and the mind of the Christian to live in such a
way on earth as to one day stand before Christ.

Newman greatly appreciated the richness of the Church's liturgical year, which unfolds before the Christian the mystery of
Christ's life—it is structured with the seasons of Advent, Christmas, Lent, Easter, and Ordinary time. His friend John Keble published *A Christian Year*, a beautiful collection of poems offering
Christians a wealth of considerations on the graces offered in
these holy seasons. Years later, some of the volumes of Newman's
Parochial and Plain Sermons collected his sermons for the various
seasons of the year.[10]

---

[8] John Henry Newman, *Parochial and Plain Sermons, Vol. 1: 1–2* (London: Longmans,
Green, and Co., 1907). From here on PPS.

[9] *PPS*, Vol. 1:5.

[10] For a rich selection of excerpts from Newman's homilies, see John Hulsman, *The Rule
of Our Warfare* (New York: Scepter Publishers, 2003).

As we would expect, Christian worship leads to holiness of life. In addition to a Calvinist and Evangelical inspiration, Newman was also inspired early on by a book by William Law, titled *A Serious Call to Holiness and Devotion*, written in 1728, which developed the Christian idea of giving glory to God through one's daily occupations, the exercise of prayer and humility.[11]

Many saints and major Christian writers teach us about holiness in everyday life, although some through their writing and preaching, such as St. Francis de Sales, St. Thérèse of Lisieux, and St. Josemaría Escrivá,[12] have insisted more on this truth. The same should be said about Blessed John Henry Newman.

Religion should be something all-important and central to a person's life—not something external and routine, but a body of truths to be studied and applied to daily life. Holiness translates into a real love for God that enlivens every work and activity, something Newman liked to refer to as "earnestness" in religion. His sermons abound with references to living the Christian virtues in imitation of Jesus and the saints. In addition to the virtues of faith, hope, and love, he insisted on piety, humility, obedience, fortitude, and perseverance.

In two sermons, *The Vanity of Human Glory* and *The Praise of Men*, Newman cautioned people on seeking human praise above the praise of God:

> When we love a person, we cannot but wish he should love us; but he cannot love us, without also feeling respect and

---

[11] William Law (1686-1761) was an Anglican clergyman distinguished for his piety and learning, who suffered the loss of his position at Cambridge for not taking an oath of allegiance to the first Hanoverian King since he had previously given his allegiance to the House of Stuart. Some important ideas in his book are reminiscent of those of two earlier Catholic saints, St. Philip Neri and St. Francis de Sales, and of later ones mentioned in this book.

[12] St. Josemaría Escrivá repeatedly teaches that holiness consists in the lifelong sanctification of one's work and relationships with others. He underlines the belief that sanctification of work in the middle of the world gives glory to God, a teaching also expressed by Newman in the sermon "Doing Glory to God in Pursuits of the World." See *PPS, Vol. 8*, 154-171. In the sermon "Passionately Loving the World," Escrivá outlines the novel concept that everyday life and material realities are the place for a Christian's encounter with God and for exercising faith, hope and charity. See *Conversations with St. Josemaría Escrivá*, (Princeton: Scepter Publishers, 2002), 175-186.

esteem towards us. And as to the question, from whom we should desire praise, and how far, we have this simple rule— from all who stand to us in Christ's place. Christ Himself is our great Judge; from Him we must supremely seek praise; and as far as men are in His place, so far may we seek it from men. We may desire the praise of our parents and superiors, and the praise of good men—in a word, all whom we have a value for; but the desire of indiscriminate praise, the praise of those for whom we have no respect or regard, this is the mischief.[13]

The sermons invite the listener or reader to take seriously the practice of virtue in everyday life; this is the holiness desired by God. It does not entail uncommon feats, rather the accomplishment of one's duties.

A distinctive aspect of Newman's teaching on holiness is found in its application to university life. His feeling was that religious faith and worship should go hand in hand with intellectual pursuits. Holiness, thus, is not a path only for those with little or no formal education.

It is telling that soon after the opening of the Catholic University of Ireland, the rector helped to design and had built a university church for the faculty and students. The ornate church was aptly dedicated to the Virgin Mary under the title of Our Lady, Seat of Wisdom. This church became the center of the religious and academic life of the university. There, during 1856 and 1857, Newman delivered eight sermons. In the first one, preached on the feast of St. Monica, he compared the university to a mother who cares solicitously for her children:

Thus while professing all sciences, and speaking by the mouths of philosophers and sages, a University delights in the well-known appellation of "Alma Mater." She is a mother who, after the pattern of that greatest and most heavenly of

[13] John Henry Newman, *PPS*, Vol. 8, 180.

mothers, is, on the one hand, "Mater Amabilis," and "Causa nostræ lætitiæ," and on the other, "Sedes Sapientiæ."[14]

In another sermon, he reminded the students what true wisdom is:

> For us, my dear Brethren, whose duties lie in this seat of learning and science, may we never be carried away by any undue fondness for any human branch of study, so as to be forgetful that our true wisdom, and nobility, and strength, consist in the knowledge of Almighty God. Nature and man are our studies, but God is higher than all. It is easy to lose Him in His works. It is easy to become over-attached to our own pursuit, to substitute it for religion, and to make it the fuel of pride.[15]

Just as St. Thomas More is a model of holiness for lawyers and statesmen, St. Gianna Baretta for physicians and mothers, St. Bernard for monks, St. Isidore for farmers, and St. Joseph for carpenters, Blessed John Henry Newman is a model of holiness for university teachers and rectors; he was both at different periods in his life, and later a teacher and principal for a boys' school. It is one thing to theorize about sanctity and another to live it out in the nitty-gritty of daily life. Newman had to suffer many difficulties and obstacles as rector of the Catholic University of Ireland. He persevered in this work for six years, practicing charity with those who made it very difficult for him to carry out his work and who, in the end, made it necessary for him to resign. During that time, he exercised the virtue of magnanimity required to begin such an enterprise and practiced understanding and generosity with students and faculty.

The inner thoughts and sentiments of Newman grew in a crescendo of love evident in the texts of short meditations published

---

[14] John Henry Newman, *Sermons Preached on Various Occasions*, [1874] (London: Longmans, Green, and Co., 1908), 5. From here on *OS*.
[15] *OS*, 29.

posthumously. These brief meditations reveal the intimate and humble relationship the author had with God, whom He addressed as *My Maker, My Savior, the Beautiful One,* etc. The prayers are doctrinal and scriptural, beginning with the recognition of central truths of the faith: the mysteries of creation, the Trinity, Incarnation, Redemption, the immortality of the soul, and personal and final judgment. The author sought to praise and give thanks to the One who is All-Holy and All Merciful. In these meditations, he voiced prayers to God such as:

> My God, I adore Thee, as holy without, as well as holy within. I adore Thee as holy in all Thy works as well as in Thy own nature. No creature can approach Thy incommunicable sanctity, but Thou dost approach, and touch, and compass, and possess, all creatures; and nothing lives but in Thee, and nothing hast Thou created but what is good.[16]

But there is nothing cold or distant in them; in this prayer Newman asked God to bathe his soul and to give him to drink of his grace:

> O mighty God, strengthen me with Thy strength, console me with Thy everlasting peace, soothe me with the beauty of Thy countenance; enlighten me with Thy uncreated brightness; purify me with the fragrance of Thy ineffable holiness. Bathe me in Thyself, and give me to drink, as far as mortal man may ask, of the rivers of grace which flow from the Father and the Son, the grace of Thy consubstantial, co-eternal Love.[17]

In his Anglican sermons, Newman spoke often of the holy ordinances and liturgy through which God makes man holy. In the Roman Catholic sermons and meditations, he spoke of the grace of the sacraments and union with Christ through the sacraments, especially the Holy Eucharist. It is through this direct contact with God that man is healed and made holy. And here he reminds

[16] *MD*, 375–376.
[17] *MD*, 367.

us that holiness is not a human achievement; rather, it is the mysterious interchange between the divine and the human. God makes us holy if we allow him to mold us and draw us to him:

> I come to Thee, O Lord, not only because I am unhappy without Thee, not only because I feel I need Thee, but because Thy grace draws me on to seek Thee for Thy own sake, because Thou art so glorious and beautiful. I come in great fear, but in greater love. O may I never lose, as years pass away, and the heart shuts up, and all things are a burden, let me never lose this youthful, eager, elastic love of Thee.[18]

Newman spoke of the "Great Presence" of God reserved as the Blessed Sacrament in Catholic churches. In his novel, *Loss and Gain* (1848), before the hero converts we find him kneeling in a church during benediction with the Blessed Sacrament. He is before that "Great Presence, which makes a Catholic church different from every other place in the world."[19] After his own conversion, Newman was deeply moved by the reservation of the Blessed Sacrament in the tabernacle of Catholic churches. He wrote his friend Henry Wilberforce:

> I am writing next room to the Chapel—It is such an incomprehensible blessing to have Christ in bodily presence in one's house, within one's walls, as swallows up all other privileges . . . To know that he is close by—to be able again and again through the day to go in to Him. (LD XI, 252).

For Newman, the Sacrament of Penance or Confession was another privileged encounter with Christ. He recalled the first confession that he heard as an Anglican clergyman in 1838, that of a young man preparing to receive the Holy Eucharist. A few years later, he wrote his friend John Keble about the heavy responsibility in a parish to remind people about confession, without which the pastoral work is shallow. Then, after resigning as vicar of the

---

[18] *MD*, 411–412.
[19] John Henry Newman, *Loss and Gain* (London: Longmans, Green, and Co., 1906), 427.

University Church, St. Mary the Virgin, he confided in one of his sisters:

> If there were no other reason in the world, why I should not undertake a parochial cure in our Church, this alone would suffice, for the future that there is no confession. I cannot understand how a clergyman can be answerable for souls, if souls are not admitted to him. There is *no real* cure of *souls* in our Church. . . (LD IX, 175, 523).

Although all of Newman's spiritual teaching was lived out in the daily relations and tasks of life, his sacramental spirituality had as its focus the world to come. Newman very often pointed in his sermons and meditations to God who reigns in heaven. For him, we are surrounded by an invisible world, the supernatural, and our goal is to prepare for the fullness of life in the celestial banquet with Christ. Holiness begins here on earth, but it is a participation of the divine life and tends to heaven where the union with the All-Holy God is realized. Newman did not present an original teaching on this point, but his writings and preaching stand out for the clarity of exposition on these truths and his insistence throughout.

And as in the case of many saints, his preaching and works were the fruit of a lived experience of holiness. Archbishop Jean Honoré elegantly describes this reality:

> All of Newman's thought draws its truth and its comprehensiveness from the depth of his own spiritual experience. If Newman is a philosopher and a theologian, an orator and a historian, it is only because he is first a spiritual man, a man of God, for whom the only thing that matters is dialogue with the Creator.[20]

Holiness is, in sum, the fullness of Christian life, the action of the Holy Spirit and the fruits of God's grace, reached through prayer

---

[20] Jean Honoré, *The Spiritual Journey of Newman* (New York: Alba House, 1992) 229.

and the sacraments and manifest in the exercise of the virtues. It is the vocation of every Christian, something attractive and fulfilling at the reach of everyone. As such, it is to be shared with others. Newman is fully conscious that this holiness desired by God is to be conveyed to others, and he prays to him:

> Stay with me, and then I shall begin to shine as Thou shinest: so to shine as to be a light to others. The light, O Jesus, will be all from Thee. None of it will be mine. No merit to me. It will be Thou who shinest through me upon others.[21]

These sentiments voiced in his prayers and the reflections expressed in his sermons shed light on the story of Newman's life as a faithful priest, a good father to his Oratory community, a generous adviser to countless people, and an exceptional scholar and teacher. Louis Bouyer closes his excellent biography of Newman with a story of the visit Jemima, Newman's sister, paid to her brother at Edgbaston. She brought with her a little grandson, and the boy, encouraged by the aged Cardinal Newman, asked what he had on his mind: "Which is greater, a Cardinal or a Saint?" The reply was, "Cardinals belong to this world, and Saints to heaven."[22] He did not think himself a saint. In fact, saints think of themselves as ordinary men and sinners. Because they see themselves in God's radiant light, they are humble and allow the radiance of God to shine through them to others.

---

[21] *MD*, 365.
[22] Louis Bouyer, *Newman, His Life and Spirituality: An Intellectual and Spiritual Biography of John Henry Newman* (San Francisco: Ignatius Press, 2011), 426.

Four

MEDITATION AND STUDY
OF THE SCRIPTURES

Once he became a Catholic, Newman would say that the Bible was everything for English Protestants and that if it were taken away from them, they would be left with nothing. While respecting Protestant devotion and reliance on the Bible, he appreciated more fully the role of the Church in the authoritative interpretation of difficult passages. In this chapter, I wish to indicate the central place the Scriptures held in Newman's life and preaching and to show that he accepted the contributions of a moderate historical and literary method in the study of the Bible that did not contradict doctrinal confessions. In this chapter, we will also suggest that his teachings on the relationship between Tradition and Scripture, on the composition of the Bible, and on biblical inspiration foreshadowed the teachings of the Constitution *Dei Verbum* (1965) of Vatican II.

In his youth and early adult life, Newman's understanding of the Scriptures was influenced by his Evangelical friends and by a few Calvinist books that he had read.[1] For instance, he accepted a literal reading of predestination to salvation, a separation of men into two classes, good and evil, and the identification of the Church of Rome as the whore of Babylon. He imbibed this false

---

[1] Newman recalled reading a work by William Romaine (1714-1795). Except for reference to the Calvinist doctrine of predestination, Newman did not remember the title nor content of the book. See *Apo.*, 4. Romaine was a well-known Anglican clergyman, preacher, and writer who had undergone an evangelical conversion in 1748.

view of the Catholic Church from the writing of Newton on biblical prophecies.[2]

But as he began to read the early Church fathers, he came to
adopt their exegesis of many scriptural truths.[3] It was a gradual
process leading to his acceptance of the ancient practice of prayer
for the souls of the dead and the authority of Peter established by
Christ, and to dispel the distorted vision of the Church of Rome.

Newman was enamored with the Word of God. He studied it
and reflected on it in order to understand its meaning. He ap-
proached the mystery that enveloped it with a humble disposition
and often acknowledged that some passages were beyond our understanding. He was careful not to dismiss these texts and, instead, accepted them with faith.

His exegesis took into account both the literal and figurative
meaning of scriptural passages. It was a spiritual and sacramental
reading of the Bible rooted in the church fathers. He was not a
biblical scholar in the way we understand biblical scholarship today. Besides Latin, he did not have a good knowledge of Greek or
Hebrew, yet his knowledge of the Bible was extraordinary in its
depth and extension. For some time, he even committed to memory large parts of the New Testament. He thus drew on numerous
doctrinal and spiritual truths from his reading and meditation of
the Bible.

Already early in 1838, in his *Lectures on Justification*, Newman
demonstrated knowledge of critical biblical exegesis, which he
criticized based on a patristic distinction between words (or *signs*)
and things. He thought the interpreter of St. Paul's Epistles should

---

[2] See Apo., 7. Sir Isaac Newton (1643-1727), the famous astronomer, was also a philosopher and theologian. His literal interpretation of the Bible led him to conclude that the
pope was the Antichrist predicted by Daniel, St. Paul, and St. John; to condemn the
Church of Rome as the whore of Babylon of the Book of Revelation; and to calculate the
date of the end of the world. These ideas were put forth in his posthumous work, *Observations upon the Prophecies of Daniel and the Apocalypse of St. John* (1733).

[3] At the age of 15, Newman had already caught an enchanting glimpse of the writings of
the church fathers, among them St. Augustine, when reading Joseph Milner's *Church History of the Church of Christ* (1794-1809)—ironically, at the same time he read Newton.

not be misled by the many senses a single word can have, looking beyond the sign to the thing signified.[4] He wrote,

> Our duty is to be intent on things, not on names and terms; to associate words with their objects, instead of measuring them by their definitions.[5]

He was equally concerned with the rise of historical criticism, in particular that the interpreter should be governed by the context of a passage of Scripture alone. He was protesting against "the bondage of modern systems" that interpret according to a theory in such a way that,

> [t]he words of Scripture are robbed of their hidden treasures, and frittered away among a multitude of meanings as uncertain, meagre, and discordant.[6]

Newman looked to the Church fathers for guidance in the interpretation of the Scriptures, rather than to modern biblical criticism.[7] He thought that the words of Scripture would be best interpreted using the "dictionary" of the Fathers.

In his seminal work, *Development of Christian Doctrine,* published in 1845, Newman held that the mystical or spiritual interpretation of Scripture had always rightly superseded the literal and that this was in fact a sign of continuity in the Church.[8] The mystical reading includes three senses: the allegorical, by which things of the Old Testament point to ones in the New Testament; the moral sense, by which Christ's actions and those who prefigured him show us what we are to do; and the anagogical sense, which signifies what lies ahead in eternal glory. Newman indicat-

---

[4] Jeffrey W. Barbeau, "Newman and the Interpretation of Inspired Scripture," *Theological Studies* 63 (2002), 62. Website: http://cdn.theologicalstudies.net/63/63.1/63.1.3.pdf.

[5] John Henry Newman, *Lectures on the Doctrine of Justification* (London: Longmans, Green, and Co., 1892), 121.

[6] *Lectures on the Doctrine of Justification*, 120.

[7] See Barbeau, 64.

[8] See John Henry Newman, *An Essay on the Development of Christian Doctrine* (1845/1878) (London: Longmans, Green, and Co., 1903), 338–346. From here on *Dev.*

ed errors that arose from a literal interpretation of Scripture, and asserted, "[i]t may be almost laid down as an historical fact, that the mystical interpretation and orthodoxy will stand or fall together."[9]

All of his sermons were thoroughly based on the Bible's transmitting to an audience the truths of the faith contained in the Word of God. It could be said of his sermons what Peter Brown wrote of St. Augustine's: "In one sermon, he could move through the whole Bible, from Paul to Genesis and back again, *via* the Psalms, piling half-verse on half-verse."[10] Although, unlike other great saints, he did not write commentaries on the books of Scripture, he touched on a wide variety of doctrinal and moral truths derived from Scripture.

In 1851, the first synod, following the reinstatement of the Roman Catholic hierarchy in England, assigned to Newman—then Father Newman—the project of a new translation of the Bible into nineteenth century English. Prior to this, there existed the Douay-Rheims Bible, a sixteenth-century English translation of the Latin Vulgate, which in the seventeenth century Bishop Richard Challoner revised, taking as its base text the King James Bible. When Cardinal Nicholas Wiseman communicated this mission to Newman, he assembled a team of translators and began work on this major project. Newman was very well prepared for this task because of his knowledge of the Scriptures, his previous work with translations from Latin to English, and his close contact with scholars in Hebrew and Greek. But William Faber, who wished for the London Oratory to undertake the project instead, urged Cardinal Wiseman to withhold the necessary support. Thus, after spending considerable time and money on this work, Newman ceased his efforts on the project, and no new translation was carried out.

---

[9] *Dev.*, 344.
[10] Peter Brown, *Augustine of Hippo, a Biography* (Berkeley: University of California Press, 2000), 251.

Newman on Biblical Inspiration and Composition

Despite this sad event in Newman's life, he would make a contribution to the study of the Bible, which foreshadowed some of the teaching of Vatican II. The council fathers of Vatican II called for a renewal of the study of Sacred Scripture and an understanding of its centrality in the teaching of theology: what the soul is to the body is what the Word of God should be for theology. They also established a three-year cycle of Sunday Mass readings to allow for reading most of the New Testament every three years.

As noted earlier, the Bible was the foundation for Newman's spiritual life and for his preaching. Through his example and sermons, he fostered among clergy and laity a similar reverence and desire to study the Bible. Over the years, he also reflected on the role of the human authors of the Scriptures, contributing to a better understanding of biblical inspiration.

From early correspondence with his brother Charles, who had become an agnostic, it seems clear that Newman was aware of disputed questions regarding authorship of the various books of Scripture, the interpolation of words into translations of the Bible, as well as slight errors in copies. These matters, he explained to his brother, did not invalidate the fact of divine revelation or the claims of the Anglican Church.

This exchange with his brother on the inspiration of the Bible, as well as its historicity and further study of these questions, became the subject of two texts: *Tract* 85 and his essay *On the Inspiration of Scripture.*[11]

Anticipating by many years some of the teachings of Vatican II's Constitution *Dei Verbum*, he put forth in these texts what the Catholic Church teaches about Sacred Scripture: the Bible is the Word of God, consigned to writing by human authors inspired by God; Sacred Tradition and Sacred Scripture form one common

---

[11] John Henry Newman, *On the Inspiration of Scripture*, in *The Nineteenth Century*, (1884), Vol. 15:84. Afterwards *On Inspiration*.

source or sacred deposit of revelation; the human authors and all parts of the books they wrote are inspired; inspiration refers in a special manner to matters of faith and doctrine; and the Church— in the person of the pope—is the authentic or authoritative interpreter of the content of this revelation.

In 1835, he wrote *Tract 85*, originally titled *Lectures on the Scripture Proofs of the Doctrines of the Church*. He argued that nowhere did the New Testament claim that it was inspired.[12] This argument was intended to show that the Bible was not self-sufficient and needed the Church for its validation. In the same tract, he commented further on the role of the human authors of the books of Scripture.

The period between this first text and the later one by Newman on the same subject saw the growth of historical literary criticism of the Bible which, in general, tended to put into doubt the historicity of both the Old and New Testaments due to historical inaccuracies and literary analyses that contradicted earlier beliefs on the composition of the books of the Bible. A feature of this method of exegesis was the denial of biblical miracles, replacing their supernatural character with natural explanations. Related to this, various "lives" of Christ were published that denied the historicity of the Gospels and questioned Christ's divinity. Examples included those by Joseph Ernest Renan and David Friedrich Strauss. In England, a collection of articles, *Essays and Reviews*, published in 1860, followed suit.

A Newman scholar suggests that in the period that ensued, Newman showed an increasing openness to the results of scientific and historical criticism.[13] Without using this term, Newman may have accepted the contributions of what we might call a moderate historical-literary criticism of the Bible that kept intact the doctrine on the divinity of Christ and the historicity of the Bible, while he recognized the need to privilege a spiritual reading of the

---

[12] St. Paul's teaching about the inspiration of the Scriptures in *2 Tim* 3:16-17 is a reference to the Old Testament, the New Testament only then in the process of composition.

[13] See J. Derek Holmes, "Newman's Attitude towards Historical Criticism and Biblical Inspiration," *Downside Review* 89 (1971) 22-37.

Scriptures within the Tradition of the Church. This openness is suggested by his 1884 essay titled *On the Inspiration of Scripture.* In this essay, published in the February issue of the *Nineteenth Century,* he put forth the Church's teachings on the inspiration and interpretation of the Bible, as well as some of his thoughts on the contribution of the inspired human authors. That May, he published a rebuttal to a harsh and unfair criticism of his essay by John Healy, an Irish seminary professor.

Newman's concern was to assist faithful Catholic scholars who were engaged in biblical studies:

> I am indeed desirous of investigating for its own sake the limit of free thought consistently with the claims upon us of Holy Scripture; still my especial interest in the inquiry is from my desire to assist those religious sons of the Church who are engaged in biblical criticism and its attendant studies, and have a conscientious fear of transgressing the rule of faith; men who wish to ascertain how far certain religion puts them under obligations and restrictions in their reasonings and inferences on such subjects, what conclusions may and what may not be held without interfering with that internal assent which they are bound to give, if they would be Catholics, to the written Word of God.[14]

He summed up the question before a biblical scholar and succinctly stated the doctrine on the authority and inspiration of the Scriptures:

> Now then, the main question before us being what it is that a Catholic is free to hold about Scripture in general, or about its separate portions or its statements, without compromising his firm inward assent to the dogmas of the Church, that is, to the *de fide* enunciations of Pope and councils, we have first of all to inquire how many and what those dogmas are.
>
> I answer that there are two such dogmas; one relates to the authority of Scripture, the other to its interpretation. As to

---

[14] On *Inspiration,* 187.

the authority of Scripture, we hold it to be, in all matters of faith and morals, divinely inspired throughout; as to its interpretation, we hold that the Church is, in faith and morals, the one infallible expounder of that inspired text.

In doing so, Newman affirmed the teaching of the Council of Trent, reiterated by Vatican I, that the Catholic Church is the sole infallible interpreter in matters of faith and morals in questions of interpretation of the Scriptures. He addressed the problem of private judgment of the Bible, which for three centuries had affected the interpretation of the Scriptures.

> How are private readers satisfactorily to distinguish what is didactic and what is historical, what is fact and what is vision, what is allegorical and what is literal, what is idiomatic and what is grammatical, what is enunciated formally and what occurs *obiter* (in passing), or what is only of temporary or of lasting obligation? Such is our natural anticipation, and it is only too exactly justified in the events of the last three centuries, in the many countries where private judgment on the text of Scripture has prevailed. The gift of inspiration requires as its complement the gift of infallibility.[15]

With regard to the doctrine on inspiration of the Scriptures, Newman noted that the Council of Trent established the canon of inspired books. Vatican Council I specified that all parts of each book were divinely inspired. In Newman's words, "The Vatican Council speaks more distinctly, saying that the entire books with all their parts, are divinely inspired, and adding an anathema upon impugners of this definition."

Vatican II, the next ecumenical council, issued *Dei Verbum*, an important constitution on revelation and the Bible (1965). The composition of this text was a delicate and complicated process that required the hard work of a group of bishops and theologians the entire period of Vatican II.[16] The authors reached a consensus,

---

[15] On *Inspiration*, 190.

[16] See Vicente Balaguer for an analysis of the different drafts of the document and the main questions debated, "La Constitución Dogmática *Dei Verbum*" in *Annuarium Historiae Conciliorum* 43 (2011), 31-71.

ratified by the council fathers, concerning difficult questions about the meaning of Tradition, the understanding of biblical inspiration and inerrancy, and the work of the inspired authors. It would be anachronistic to think that Newman answered questions posed a century later by the Council fathers. Nonetheless, although his immediate context was different, he dealt with similar questions and the criticism leveled by rationalist thinkers, and he offered convincing solutions.

In the preparation of *Dei Verbum*, there was significant debate on the relationship of the understanding of Sacred Tradition and its relation to Scripture. Is everything in Scripture in Tradition? In other words, is Scripture materially sufficient? Yves Congar, who knew the writings of Newman well and was one of the theologians that drafted *Dei Verbum*, drew from Newman, J. Möhler, M. Scheeben, and J. Franzelin the notion that the two sources, Tradition and Scripture, form one whole.[17]

In the final text of the constitution we read to this effect:

Hence there exists a close connection and communication between Sacred Tradition and Sacred Scripture. For both of them, flowing from the same divine wellspring, in a certain way merge into a unity and tend towards the same end.[18]

In the same section, drafted by Congar and a few others, there are also some words about the development of Tradition in which Congar takes from Newman's fifteenth *Oxford University Sermon* the example of the Virgin Mary as "our pattern of Faith." Thus in *Dei Verbum* we read:

This tradition which comes from the Apostles develops in the Church with the help of the Holy Spirit. For there is a growth in the understanding of the realities and the words which have been handed down. This happens through a contemplation and study made by believers, who treasure these things in

---

[17] Andrew Meszaros, *Haec Traditio proficit*: Congar's Reception of Newman in *Dei Verbum*, Section 8, *New Black Friars*, 92 (2011), 247-254.

[18] Paul VI, Dogmatic Constitution on Divine Revelation *Dei Verbum* (November 18, 1965), n. 9.

their hearts (see Luke, 2:19, 51) through a penetrating under-standing of the spiritual realities which they experience, and through the preaching of those who have received through episcopal succession the sure gift of truth.[19]

The constitution *Dei Verbum* repeated and cited the teachings of St. Augustine, St. Jerome, St. Thomas Aquinas, and two encycli-cals on the Bible, *Providentissimus Deus* (1893) and *Divino Af-flante Spiritu* (1943). It did not mention Newman although its content is very similar to that written by him eighty years earlier. It is true that Newman supported his arguments on the testimony of Augustine and Thomas, but he added to it with his clarity of exposition and arguments drawn from the Councils of Trent and Vatican I. It is possible that besides Congar, those who worked on the commission that drafted *Dei Verbum* had read Newman's essay on the inspiration of the Scriptures, yet he is not cited in the foot-notes of the text and only figures once in the corresponding sec-tion of the important *Commentary on the Documents of Vatican II*.[20] In various other works on the documents of Vatican II, his name appears in a footnote or does not appear at all.[21] The reason for this absence of Newman's views may be that he was not as well known outside the English-speaking world, or, more likely, that his work was mistakenly considered too partial to the historical-critical method, or even heretical.[22]

A case in point is how Newman forthrightly addressed the sub-ject of what Christians must believe about those matters in the Bible that do not touch directly on questions of faith and morals. He asked: What should Christians believe about the inspiration of "matters of fact"?

[19] *Dei Verbum*, n. 8.
[20] Herbert Vorgrimler General Ed., *Commentary of the Documents of Vatican II*, Vol. III (New York: Herder and Herder, 1969).
[21] See *History of Vatican II*, Vol. II, *The Formation of the Council's Identity*, ed. Giuseppe Alberigo. English version, ed. Joseph A. Komonchak, (Orbis: Maryknoll, 1997), 386, foot-note 49. Another commentary, *Vatican II Forty Years Later*, ed. William Madges, (2011), does not mention Newman.
[22] See Barbeau, 67.

But while the councils, as has been shown, lay down so emphatically the inspiration of Scripture in respect to 'faith and morals,' it is remarkable that they do not say a word directly as to inspiration in matters of fact. Yet, are we therefore to conclude that the record of facts in Scripture does not come under the guarantee of its inspiration? We are not so to conclude, and for this plain reason—the sacred narrative carried on through so many ages, what is it but the very matter for our faith and rule of our obedience? What but that narrative itself is the supernatural teaching, in order to which inspiration is given? What is the whole history, traced out in Scripture from Genesis to Esdras and thence on to the end of the Acts of the Apostles, but a manifestation of Divine Providence, on the one hand interpretative, on a large scale and with analogical applications, of universal history; and on the other preparatory, typical and predictive, of the Evangelical Dispensation?[23]

At the end of this long passage, Newman clearly upheld the inspiration of all the parts of the books of the Bible, not only those that pertain directly to faith and morals:

> In this point of view it has God for its author, even though the finger of God traced no words but the Decalogue. Such is the claim of Bible history in its substantial fulness (sic) to be accepted de fide as true. In this point of view, Scripture is inspired, not only in faith and morals, but in all its parts which bear on faith, including matters of fact.[24]

Newman continued, explaining that, given the complexity of the Bible, its composition by many authors at different times and places, and its obscure passages, it requires an infallible interpreter, and such a one is the pope. According to the Council of Trent, the pope is the authoritative interpreter. He is the infallible inter-

[23] *On Inspiration*, 49.
[24] Ibid, 50.

preter, but, until he formally interprets a passage, there is nothing heretical in advocating a contrary interpretation as long as there is nothing in it inconsistent with the faith, contrary to piety, offensive, or scandalous.

After all this, Newman explained his position simply, asserting that the Bible is the Word of God, which "cannot be put on the level of other books." In sum, Newman offered a criticism of rationalism in exegesis, which scarcely ten years later would be strongly voiced by Pope Leo XIII in *Providentissimus Deus*:

> Such then is the answer which I make to the main question which has led to my writing. I asked what obligation of duty lay upon the Catholic scholar or man of science as regards his critical treatment of the text and the matter of Holy Scripture. And now I say that it is his duty, first, never to forget that what he is handling is the Word of God, which, by reason of the difficulty of always drawing the line between what is human and what is divine, cannot be put on the level of other books, as it is now the fashion to do, but has the nature of a Sacrament, which is outward and inward, and a channel of supernatural grace; and secondly, that, in what he writes upon it or its separate books, he is bound to submit himself internally, and to profess to submit himself, in all that relates to faith and morals, to the definite teachings of Holy Church.[25]

At the same time that Newman underlined the supernatural character of the Bible, which he likened to a sacrament, he encouraged Catholic scholars who did historical and linguistic studies of the Bible. The magisterial teaching that came after Newman did likewise, notably the encyclical *Divino Afflante Spiritu*.

Newman's essays make other important contributions. One of these is to lend weight to the thinking advanced by others before him, regarding the composition of given books of Scripture by more than one author and at different periods of time. According

---

[25] On *Inspiration*, 192.

to him, the human authors could be called the "immediate editors" of a book. Such would be the case with Jason of Cyrene for the First Book of Maccabees, and St. Luke for the Gospel that bears his name. Newman wrote:

> Again, it follows from there being two agencies, divine grace and human intelligence, co-operating in the production of the Scriptures, that, whereas, if they were written, as in the Decalogue, by the immediate finger of God, every word of them must be His and His only, on the contrary, if they are man's writing, informed and quickened by the presence of the Holy Ghost, they admit, should it so happen, of being composed of outlying materials, which have passed through the minds and from the fingers of inspired penmen, and are known to be inspired on the ground that those who were the immediate editors, as they may be called, were inspired.[26]

From this, Newman concluded with a passage that is reminiscent of the teaching in *Dei Verbum* about the composition of the Sacred Scriptures[27]:

> Hence we have no reason to be surprised, nor is it against the faith to hold, that a canonical book may be composed, not only from, but even of, pre-existing documents, it being always borne in mind, as a necessary condition, that an inspired mind has exercised a supreme and an ultimate judgment on the work, determining what was to be selected and embodied in it, in order to its truth in all 'matters of faith and morals pertaining to the edification of Christian doctrine,' and its unadulterated truth.[28]

---

[26] On *Inspiration*, 194.

[27] See *Dei Verbum*, n. 19: "(. . .) The sacred authors wrote the four Gospels, selecting some things from the many which had been handed on by word of mouth or in writing, reducing some of them to a synthesis, explaining some things in view of the situation of their churches and preserving the form of proclamation but always in such fashion that they told us the honest truth about Jesus."

[28] On *Inspiration*, 195.

Newman also addressed the subject of the inspiration of nonessential historical matters in Scripture. He put forward the question of whether these "matters of fact," such as "the wagging of the tail of Tobias' dog" (Tb 11:9), or "the cloak left by St. Paul at Troas with Carpus" (2 Tim 4:13), fall under the guarantee of divine inspiration. Newman called these matters *obiter dicta*, that is, things which are said "in passing" or "by the way," as opposed to matters of faith and morals.[29] He was inclined to think that they do not fall under the scope of inspiration but submitted this to the teaching of the Church. He did not equate this with error but rather with something one is not bound to believe literally unless defined by the Church. Newman explained that according to St. Thomas: "In all matters which Scripture delivers after the manner of historical narrative, we must hold, as a fundamental fact, the truth of the history." He seemed to differ, however, with St. Augustine and St. Thomas, who preferred to interpret a passage in a spiritual sense when they found some historical inaccuracy.

Leo XIII in *Providentissimus Deus*, and Pius XII in *Divino Afflante Spiritu*, presented inspiration tied to the concept of inerrancy, something which Paul VI and the council fathers of Vatican II chose not to do, presenting inspiration instead in a positive manner—that is, expressing what it is rather than what it is not.[30] For this reason the encyclical letters mentioned above rejected as erroneous the concept of obiter *dicta* which, according to these encyclicals, would be tantamount to errors in Scripture.[31] However, as noted, Newman did not consider these words or passages

---

[29] Newman defined *obiter dicta* in the Scriptures as follows: "by obiter dicta being meant phrases, clauses, or sentences in Scripture about matters of mere fact, which, as not relating to faith and morals, may without violence be referred to the human element in its composition."

[30] See Balaguer, 31-71.

[31] See Pius XII, *Divino Afflante Spiritu*, (1943), nn. 1 and 38. In n. 38, the encyclical reads: "Not infrequently—to mention only one instance—when some persons reproachfully charge the Sacred Writers with some historical error or inaccuracy in the recording of facts, on closer examination it turns out to be nothing else than those customary modes of expression and narration peculiar to the ancients, which used to be employed in the mutual dealings of social life and which in fact were sanctioned by common usage." Also Leo XIII, *Providentissimus Deus*, (1893), nn. 20 and 21.

as errors in Scripture; rather, they were *dicta* that do not fall under the scope of inspiration because they are minute matters that do not require inspiration and do not bear on matters of faith and morals.

A longer study of Newman's teaching on the Bible would take us to his sermons, which reveal a deep meditation and understanding of the Bible as the inspired Word of God. For him, the study and understanding of the Bible required a look at the whole of Scripture and belief in doctrinal truths put forth by the creeds and other confessions of faith. And this study, he felt, should privilege the spiritual and allegorical meaning, guided by the church fathers and the authoritative interpretation of the Church's hierarchy.

With this overview of Newman's approach to the Bible, we can appreciate the impetus he gave to meditation and study of the Word of God. In like manner, we can recognize in his writings important ideas on the relationship between Tradition and Sacred Scripture, and on the composition and inspiration of the books of Scripture that are present in *Dei Verbum.*

Five

THE MORAL LIFE IN THE KINGDOM OF GOD

A moral life consists in the practice of what is good, which man can know through reason aided by the light of faith, and the Church's teaching. For Jews and Christians, the moral life is summed up in the practice of the Commandments and Beatitudes. There is nothing new here. Throughout time, however, saints and other ecclesial writers have laid stress on certain aspects of the moral life. As Pope Benedict pointed out in the Apostolic Exhortation *Verbum Domini*, some saints have understood in a special way certain elements of Christian life: St. Francis, poverty and simplicity; St. Ignatius of Loyola, the search for truth and discernment of spirits; St. Pius of Pietralcina (Padre Pio), living as an instrument of divine Mercy; and St. Josemaría Escrivá, the universal call to holiness.[1]

Was there something specific that Newman drew from the Scriptures regarding the moral life? Like other saints, he gave special importance to the virtues of faith, hope and charity. The Christian must live by faith, not by sight. Perhaps what he emphasized most was the concept of obedience to God—the obedience of the creature to its Creator. Man responds with his intellect and his will to God's designs and commands. In sermons, Newman pointed out the example of the patriarchs and other saints—their obedience of faith—and indicated the obedience of Christ himself.

[1] See Benedict XVI, Post Synodal Exhortation *Verbum Domini* (Vatican: 2010), n. 48. St. Josemaría Escrivá did not tire of repeating that the vocation to holiness, based on the baptismal consecration, should not be relegated—in the thought of many—solely to the life of priests and religious, as has been the case for many centuries. Newman, too, localized the basis for the Christian vocation in Baptism, and Christ's threefold mission: to sanctify, to teach and to rule.

Consequently, he stressed man's accountability before God's throne. His sermons always pointed to our Lord's Second Coming, recalling the parables that urge watchfulness, and presented Christ's teaching on the Last Day. Newman did not teach a religion of fear, yet he did not shy away from reminding his listeners and readers that God is the almighty Creator and Judge. If man wishes to see God one day, he must live here on earth as corresponds to a son of God. He must practice justice and righteousness. Man should live and work keeping in mind the Kingdom of God and its definitive manifestation in heaven.

In Newman's words, to watch for God is:

> To be detached from what is present, and to live in what is unseen; to live in the thought of Christ as He came once, and He will come again; to desire His second coming, from our affectionate remembrance of His first. (. . .)
>
> (Many men) have a number of good qualities, and are in a certain sense and up to certain point religious; but they do not watch. Their notion of religion is briefly this: loving God indeed, but loving this world too; not only doing their *duty*, but finding their chief and highest *good*, in that state of life to which it has pleased God to call them, resting in it, taking it as their portion. They serve God, and they seek Him; but they look on the present world as if it were eternal.[2]

Today, as in Newman's days, many people are nominally Christian. They keep the external practices of Christianity and celebrate major feasts, but their hearts do not seek to do God's will. Instead, God wants men and women to "delight in the Law" and to walk according to his ways with a sincere heart and mind. Newman's sermons were directed to convert people, to foster "earnestness" in religious practice, both in piety and morality. He criticized the social religion of the day, which considered sin an excess or bad taste rather than an offense against God, and prized tolerance instead of obedience to God. He also often indicated the folly of worldliness.

[2] John Henry Newman, *PPS*, Vol. 4, 325-326.

For Newman, the moral life is achieved through a constant effort to respond to God's grace. A Christian must practice self-denial and develop habits of prayer. The moral life is not a titanic effort to overcome disordered passions. God grants man abundant graces through the sacraments to live as his children. Referring to baptism, he wrote:

> For the new birth of the Holy Spirit sets the soul in motion in a heavenly way: it gives us good thoughts and desires, enlightens and purifies us, and prompts us to seek God. In a word (as I have said), it gives a spiritual *life*: it opens the eyes of our minds, so that we begin to see God in all things by faith, and hold continual intercourse with Him in prayer; and if we cherish these gracious influences, we shall become holier and wiser and more heavenly, year by year, our hearts being ever in a course of change from darkness to light, from the ways and works of Satan, to the perfection of Divine obedience.[3]

Newman espoused a morality of holiness. Men are called to live all the commandments and precepts of religion, but for the sake of pleasing God, who is all-good and loving, not for some servile fear of punishment. As in the parable of the ten virgins, Christians should trim their lights and be prepared for the return of their master. Happy the man whom his Lord finds ready for the wedding banquet. This fine balance between justice and piety is characteristic in Newman. God wants his children to live "in justice," yet he is kind and merciful to them.

This way of considering the moral life as obedience to a loving God who is our Creator is a healthy and appealing notion of obedience, consonant with the formulation a little more than a half century later by Romano Guardini:

> The will of God is the love of the Father. It not an impersonal law but the living, creative power of the Creator of man and the world. It is not a command issued by a sovereign to

[3] John Henry Newman, *PPS*, Vol. 7, 210.

his subjects but the personal claim of a Father on his sons and daughters. It is his loving will for the individual child of God, a living force which encourages and sustains. It is the gracious act of Love which enables to be heard and affords the power to fulfill it. It is the power of the love that gives all; it is Being, Power, and Deed.[4]

Newman did not refer as much to God as Father than as Creator, Lord, and Savior, but he did it sufficiently for us to see that he taught a morality based on love rather than strict justice; or, better yet, on a just fulfillment of God's precepts based on love. The moral life aspires to holiness; it hinges on love rather than fear.

Some twentieth-century saints develop the biblical teaching of divine sonship in its relation to the moral life. Outstanding among these are St. Thérèse of the Child Jesus, St. John Paul II, and St. Josemaría Escrivá[5] whose work was spread further by his successors Blessed Alvaro del Portillo and Bishop Javier Echevarría.

Another element that Newman highlighted in his explanation of the Church's moral teaching is the beauty and goodness of God's commands, and of God himself. A Christian is drawn to God by means of the attraction exerted by Christ, the splendor of the Father. It is his beauty and goodness that attracts, more than the fear of pain and loss. In one of his notes for meditation, he writes:

My Lord Jesu, I confess and know that Thou art the True, the Beautiful, and the Good. Thou alone canst make me bright and glorious, and canst lead me up after Thee. Thou art the way, the truth, and the life, and none but Thou.[6]

---

[4] Romano Guardini, *The Living God*, (New York: Pantheon Books, 1957), 42.

[5] St. Josemaría Escrivá emphasized the truth of divine filiation or sonship as the fruit of baptism. He invited Christians to go deeper into this truth everyday. For instance he wrote: "Rest in divine filiation. God is a Father—your Father!—full of warmth and infinite love. Call him Father frequently and tell him, when you are alone, that you love him, that you love him very much!, and that you feel proud and strong because you are his son. Josemaría Escrivá, *The Way, Furrow, The Forge* (single volume edition), (New York: Scepter Publishers, 2011), n. 331, p. 650.

[6] *MD*, 390.

At the same time, Newman emphasizes the role of freedom in the moral life, a freedom that relies on knowledge of the truth and the attraction that it exerts on the intellect to choose what is good. We have reason through which we can know natural and revealed truths, but in addition, we have the Church's teaching to guide and correct our choices. By means of all these channels, man is able to know and choose what is right.

The moral conscience, according to Newman in keeping with Tradition, is the voice of God, speaking to each person, reminding him to do what is right and to refrain from what is wrong. The conscience is not an excuse to do whatever one thinks or feels; it is a reminder of God's law that obliges each person to act rightly.

In an open letter to the Duke of Norfolk, Newman dedicates a chapter to the doctrine on conscience. There he writes:

> This view of conscience, I know, is very different from that ordinarily taken of it, both by the science and literature, and by the public opinion, of this day. It is founded on the doctrine that conscience is the voice of God, whereas it is fashionable on all hands now to consider it in one way or another creation of man.[7]

There is no audible voice, but it is said to be the voice of God in the sense that it is man's understanding of the natural law, which is a participation in God's eternal law or design for creation. As such, conscience has "the prerogative of commanding obedience." Newman specifies that it is the voice of God in the nature and heart of man, distinct from the voice of revelation. Man must discern the content, and revelation provides a guarantee for his conclusions. In other words, the moral conscience, according to Newman, is man's apprehension of God's law. He also calls it "a messenger from Him, who, both in nature and in grace, speaks to us behind a veil." Newman could not be clearer: the conscience does not create the law. It is, instead, an internal witness of God's Law.

---

[7] John Henry Newman, *Letter to the Duke of Norfolk*, in *Certain Difficulties Felt by Anglicans in Catholic Teaching*, Vol. 2 [1875] (London: Longmans, Green, and Co., 1900), 247. From here on *Diff.*, Vol. 2.

The conscience binds the subject, and each person must act in accord with his conscience—but precisely by a conscience that is instructed in the truth revealed by God. This is a far cry from the notion of "doing whatever one wishes" under the mistaken belief that the moral conscience is autonomous—that is, literally that it is a law unto itself. Neither conscience nor freedom should be construed as a sovereign arbiter of what is morally good or evil. Instead, it is a strong and immediate reminder of what is true. Yet the voice of conscience can be distorted, especially when someone fails to seek what God has revealed and the Church's authentic interpretation of given truths.

Modern man uses the word "conscience" as a convenient way to rationalize his sins. Wrong actions are no longer such; they are justified as "acting in conscience." Man abolishes absolute commands; there are no longer actions that are always wrong *per se*. Now, each person is free to decide "according to his own conscience." This is moral relativism dressed up in respectable language. Newman spent his life fighting this type of doctrinal and moral relativism, which he called liberalism in religion.

The *Letter to the Duke of Norfolk* points out various notions of conscience among many men who teach modern philosophy, science, or literature:

> We are told that conscience is but a twist in primitive and untutored man; that its dictate is an imagination; that the very notion of guiltiness, which that dictate enforces, is simply irrational, for how can there possibly be freedom of will, how can there be consequent responsibility, in that infinite eternal network of cause and effect, in which we helplessly lie? And what retribution have we to fear, when we have had no real choice to do good or evil?[8]

Sadly, for the average man, according to Newman, the "rights of conscience" does not mean the rights of the Creator and our duties toward him. It means our human rights to think, speak, write

[8] *Diff.*, Vol. 2, 249.

or act according to our own judgment without any regard to God. No Englishman or Western man wishes to be told what to do. He wishes to act according to his self-will, which he calls conscience.

This is a moral position foreign to Christian Tradition and to Newman's exposition of the moral conscience, especially as formulated by St. Thomas Aquinas. Thinking he was quoting Aquinas from Gousset's *Théologie Morale*, he in fact quoted St. Alphonse who, in agreement with Aquinas, wrote that "conscience is the practical judgment or dictate of reason, by which we judge what is to be done as being good, or to be avoided as evil."[9] God provides us, thus, with a practical help to make the decisions in the here and now (*hic et nunc*). The judgments of conscience conform to the teachings that God has enabled man to discover through reason alone and that are taught by the Church.

In recent times, an appeal to one's conscience has been used as a way to justify behavior contrary to both natural and revealed law, especially in matters of sexual morality and marriage. Sadly, there is almost no knowledge about the basis and limits for the moral conscience and its relation to objective moral norms, and the Church's teaching. It is of little surprise that many people will employ these words, which have a semblance of respectability, to distort an axiom in moral theology that directs people to always follow conscience as the proximate, albeit not definitive, norm of conduct in life.

How can someone appeal to his conscience to act contrary to God's law? This is a contradiction in terms, which confirms the serious lack of good doctrine as well as the degree of self-justification for behavior that defies Christ's moral teaching. The notion that in the "internal forum" (the Sacrament of Reconciliation), a priest can tell a penitent to follow the dictates of his conscience in matters of morals that go against Church teaching makes no sense. It suggests that there are two different authorities: the

---

[9] Alphonse Ligouri, *Theologia Moralis*, Part 1, Chapter 1. Website: https://archive.org/stream/theologiamorali04mansgoog#page/n84/mode/2up

Church's and one's conscience, and that in some circumstances the latter must prevail.

In a very keen exposition of Newman's teaching on conscience, Ian Ker explains how, according to Newman, conscience deals with human conduct rather than speculative truths. It decides on concrete acts of the person here and now and therefore cannot collide with papal teaching on doctrine. It may rarely collide with a command or an order given by a pope, but most of the time, such a command would fall outside the scope of papal infallibility.[10]

When closing the chapter on conscience in the *Letter to the Duke of Norfolk*, Newman offered a surprising toast. He proposed a toast for the pope but said that if he was obliged to choose, he would toast first to conscience! Here an explanation is called for. The subject of the letter was the then newly pronounced dogma of papal infallibility. Newman, who adhered to the dogma, explained that the scope of such papal pronouncements, which are infallible, is limited to matters of faith and morals. In other matters, such as prudential and political actions, the pope's judgment is not infallible. Only in infallible judgments could the pope's judgment overturn the individual's conscience. Otherwise, a properly formed conscience, rightly understood, has supreme authority because in its dictates, a person hears God's voice guiding him to act in the here and now.

This vision of the moral life: a morality of holiness, inspired by God's revelation in the Scriptures, instructed by the Church and directed by the moral conscience, constitutes the basis for Newman's preaching. It was not new teaching, yet he articulated it with great clarity and balance, presenting it in all its beauty. Oratorian Father Drew Morgan holds: "If Newman is named a 'Doctor of the Church,' it will be due in no small part to the factors that have led so many already to hold him to be the Doctor of Conscience."[11] Furthermore, John Henry Newman was an exam-

[10] Ker, *Newman on Vatican II*, pp. 116-125, p. 120 in particular.
[11] Morgan, 6.

ple of what he eloquently preached, so much so that at his beatifi-cation on September 20, 2010, Pope Benedict XVI chose to high-light his charity rather than his intellectual achievements. His charitable life was known by the Anglicans, Protestants, and Catholics alike, who lined the streets of Birmingham during his funeral procession to pay him a last tribute.

Six

A CHRISTIAN VISION OF PURSUITS IN THE WORLD

A mention of the term "world" in the writings of saints and spiritual authors was for many centuries primarily directed to warning Christians of the dangers of the pursuit of riches. Blessed Newman was keenly aware of the harm done by materialism in a Great Britain with its great prosperity and social inequality; he wrote: "[T]his most fearful earthly and groveling spirit is likely, alas! to extend itself more and more among our countrymen,—an intense, sleepless, restless, never-wearied, never-satisfied, pursuit of Mammon in one shape or other, to the exclusion of all deep, all holy, all calm, all reverent thoughts."[1] However, despite such warnings against avarice and idolatry, Newman offered laymen a vision of work in the world as the place and means through which to give glory to God. In this way he painted a positive view of human work.

He did this in various sermons but especially in one titled "Doing Glory to God in Pursuits of the World," indicating that men who seek Christian perfection and look to the final destiny of heaven may easily neglect their active duties on earth and to act for God's glory.

They are apt to wish to spend the time of their sojourning here in a positive separation from active and social duties: yet it should be recollected that the employments of this world, though not themselves heavenly, are, after all, the way to

[1] *PPS*, Vol. 8, 154-171.

heaven—though not the fruit, are the seed of immortality—
and are valuable, though not in themselves, yet for that to
which they lead: but it is difficult to realize this.[2]

Newman noted that a person who has a conversion from a disso-
lute life is more tempted to leave the common pursuits of men to
become spiritually minded.

> (. . .) and he fancies that to have a spiritual mind it is abso-
> lutely necessary to renounce all earnestness or activity in his
> worldly employments, to profess to take no interest in them,
> to despise the natural and ordinary pleasures of life, violating
> the customs of society, adopting a melancholy air and a sad
> tone of voice, and remaining silent and absent when among
> his natural friends and relatives . . .[3]

Such a person has a mistaken vision of work and professions in the
world:

> [H]e looks upon his worldly occupation simply as a burden
> and a cross, and considers it all gain to be able to throw it off;
> and the sooner he can release himself from it, and the oftener,
> so much the better.[4]

Newman did not deny that work often entails the Cross, but he
taught that through work man should serve and please God.

> The Lord Jesus Christ our Saviour is best served, and with the
> most fervent spirit, when men are not slothful in business,
> but do their duty in that state of life in which it has pleased
> God to call them.[5]

[2] *PPS*, Vol. 8, 154.
[3] *PPS*, Vol. 8, 157.
[4] *PPS*, Vol. 8, 158.
[5] *PPS*, Vol. 8, 158.

In the same sermon, Newman pointed out the error of those who think they are spiritually minded because they leave the world as a hermit would do, but in fact. . .

> . . . They do neither one thing nor the other; they neither flee it, nor engage zealously in its concerns; but they remain in the midst of them, doing them in an indolent and negligent way, and think this is to be spiritually minded.[6]

Instead, Newman argued that we can serve God without being slothful in business, and being both active and meditative in our pursuits in the world. Men err by falling into the ages-old false dichotomy between work (active life) and prayer (contemplative prayer), based on the Gospel distinction between Mary and Martha. Another stumbling block is a misunderstanding of what it means to avoid the mistakes of those who make the world their aim:

> Now what leads such a person into this mistake is, that he sees that most men who engage cheerfully and diligently in worldly business, do so from a worldly spirit, from a low carnal love of the world; and so he thinks it is his duty, on the contrary, not to take a cheerful part in the world's business at all.[7]

This common attitude of many following a religious conversion is mistaken. Men are called to take an active part in the world, fulfilling their professions cheerfully and seeking foremost to render glory to God through their work. This is the principle thread of Newman's sermon, the first motive that should animate men's work, and a central idea that he imparted on the men and women to whom he gave spiritual direction. Through their work they were called to give glory to God. Allowing that a man's occupation or circumstance may sometimes be his cross, Newman explained,

---

[6] *PPS*, Vol. 8, 160.
[7] *PPS*, Vol. 8, 159.

(. . .) that while in it he is to glorify God, not out of it, but in it, and by means of it, according to the Apostle's direction, "not slothful in business, fervent in spirit, serving the Lord." The Lord Jesus Christ our Saviour is best served, and with the most fervent spirit, when men are not slothful in business, but do their duty in that state of life in which it has pleased God to call them.[8]

Another important aspect of Newman's notion of Christian work is that by means of his work, a Christian brings others closer to God. He did not elaborate with examples from the world of work, but his thinking on this subject is found throughout his sermons in the exhortation to the practice of the moral virtues. This is the apostolic dimension of work, which is a wide and rich field open to all in whatever trade or profession:

A second reason which will animate the Christian will be a desire of letting his light shine before men. He will aim at winning others by his own diligence and activity. He will say to himself, "My parents" or "my master" or "employer shall never say of me, Religion has spoiled him. They shall see me more active and alive than before. I will be punctual and attentive, and adorn the Gospel of God our Saviour."[9]

As a foundation for his exposition on the sanctification of work, Newman looked to Christ's example.[10] The Son of God labored with his hands and in Joseph's workshop. In this and all his life a Christian must consider and follow Christ' example:

---

[8] *PPS*, Vol. 8, 158.

[9] *PPS*, Vol. 8, 163-164.

[10] Newman did not use the term "sanctification of work," one which is very frequently used by Escrivá in his writings, but he had in mind a similar idea. The latter's theology of work is in part summarized by his teaching that 'you must sanctify your work, sanctify yourself in your work, and sanctify others through your work.' In addition to placing Christ as the model for the work of a Christian, he looked to the figure of St. Joseph and often spoke of him as the model for a Christian's work. See "In Joseph's Workshop" in *Christ is Passing By*.

He [a Christian] will recollect our Saviour's life. Christ was brought up to a humble trade. When he labours in his own, he will think of his Lord and Master in His. He will recollect that Christ went down to Nazareth and was subject to His parents, that He walked long journeys, that He bore the sun's heat and the storm, and had not where to lay His head.[11]

In another sermon, "The Visible Church for the Sake of the Elect," Newman decried the "low aspirations" men are apt to have in pursuits of the world—which should not be confused with a good detachment from material goods. He explains that sin, not poverty, is the hindrance, where sin is a disordered attachment to material comforts and human praise.[12] As in other places, he admonishes against the worldly view of seeking riches.

According to the Oxford don, a Christian must act out of love for God in the ordinary duties of life, which would naturally be comprised of family and work obligations. Instead, men focus on novelties or big things. Newman asked:

Why is it that we are so open to the power of excitement? why is it that we are looking out for novelties? why is it that we complain of want of variety in a religious life? why that we cannot bear to go on in an ordinary round of duties year after year? why is it that lowly duties, such as condescending to men of low estate, are distasteful and irksome?[13]

Newman insisted, as demonstrated in an earlier chapter, that the goal of a Christian's existence should be holiness and nothing less. It cannot be the mere fullfilment of laws out of fear, and much less the love of money.

It is possible to obey, not from love towards God and man, but from a sort of conscientiousness short of love; from some

---

[11] *PPS*, Vol. 8, 164-165.
[12] See *PPS*, Vol. 4, 164.
[13] *PPS*, Vol. 5, 335-336.

notion of acting up to a law; that is, more from the fear of God than from love of Him.[14]

He strongly criticized what he called a "religion of the world" and the misunderstanding of true religion.

Man is made to love. So far is plain. They see that clearly and truly; but religion, as far as they conceive of it, is a system destitute of objects of love; a system of fear. It repels and forbids, and thus seems to destroy the proper function of man, or, in other words, to be unnatural. And it is true that this sort of fear of God, or rather slavish dread, as it may more truly be called, is unnatural; but then it is not religion, which really consists, not in the mere fear of God, but in His love; or if it be religion, it is but the religion of devils, who believe and tremble; or of idolaters, whom devils have seduced, and whose worship is superstition,—the attempt to appease beings whom they love not; and, in a word, the religion of the children of this world, who would, if possible, serve God and Mammon, and, whereas religion consists of love and fear, give to God their fear, and to Mammon their love.[15]

Still, there are many who do not aspire to worldly goods, yet neither do they aspire to heavenly ones. They become indolent; they are sucked in by the concerns of the world and live out their lives stuck in the mire.

However, the multitude of men go neither in the one way nor the other; they neither have the high ambition nor the low ambition. It is well they have not the low, certainly; it is well they do not aim at being great men, or heroes; but they have no temptation to do so. What they are tempted to, is to settle down in a satisfied way in the world as they find it, to sit down in the "mire and dirt" of their natural state, to immerse themselves and be absorbed in the unhealthy marsh which is

[14] *PPS*, Vol. 5, 331.
[15] *PPS*, Vol. 5, 332.

under them. They tend to become part of the world, and be sucked in by it, and (as it were) changed into it; and so to lose all aspirations and thoughts, whether good or bad, after any thing higher than what they are.[16]

For Newman, a Christian must work as St. Paul did for his livelihood, all the while trusting in God's providence, and always living according to a higher law. His bearing is such that in all states and conditions of life he seeks holiness.

They are not gloomy, or morose, or overbearing, or restless; but still they are pursuing in their daily walk, and by their secret thoughts and actions, a conduct above the world. Whether rich or poor, high-born or low-born, married or single, they have never wedded themselves to the world; they have never surrendered themselves to be its captives; never looked out for station, fashion, comfort, credit, as the end of life.[17]

In another sermon, "Love, the One Thing Needful," Newman indicates the need to shun a smooth and easy life so that we can love our Lord who died for us on the Cross. If we wish to grow in love for him and attain heaven, he writes, we must undeceive ourselves of the desire to avoid suffering in this life:

A smooth and easy life, an uninterrupted enjoyment of the goods of Providence, full meals, soft raiment, well-furnished homes, the pleasures of sense, the feeling of security, the consciousness of wealth,—these, and the like, if we are not careful, choke up all the avenues of the soul, through which the light and breath of heaven might come to us. A hard life is, alas! no certain method of becoming spiritually minded, but it is one out of the means by which Almighty God makes us so.[18]

[16] *PPS*, Vol. 4, 163.
[17] *PPS*, Vol. 4, 166.
[18] *PPS*, Vol. 5, 337.

In these and other passages, Newman offered some general elements for a spirituality and theology of work which would be developed in the twentieth century, in particular through the teaching and works of St. Josemaría Escrivá[19] and various other theologians such as Yves Congar and Gustave Thils, and, later, put forth by the documents of Vatican II.[20] This body of teaching presents human work in the context of the theology of creation, redemption, and eschatology as well as the path of Christian holiness.

Although Newman confined himself primarily to spiritual and moral considerations on work without formulating a theology of work, he provides his readers with a positive vision of an active and prayerful involvement in the pursuits of the world with the clear goal of giving glory to God. As we will suggest in other chapters in his work in education and in his work with professionals such as lawyers and physicians, he offered more specific advice for the achievement of this vision.

These students, professionals, and tradesmen whom Newman addressed, like Christians of all ages, had to understand religious truths and the Church's teaching and apply them to everyday life. This task brought them before the reality of the development of doctrine to which Newman applied his keen insight, and which we examine in the next chapter.

---

[19] José Luis Illanes, inspired by the teaching of Escrivá, wrote *The Sanctification of Work* (Scepter Publishers, 2003). Escrivá laid great emphasis on the ordinary life as the place of the encounter with God, and how a person's work occupies the greater part of that ordinary life. To convey this notion he coined the expression "holiness in the middle of the world."

[20] Other contributions to the idea of sanctification of earthly realities and work came from the *Jeunesse Ouvrière Chrétienne* (Christian Working Youth) founded in Belgium in 1925 by Joseph Cardijn, and a few years later from Catholic Action, founded by Pope Pius XI (1922-1939). Catholic Action promoted the participation and collaboration of the laity in the apostolate of the hierarchy, whereas Newman, and later Escrivá, emphasized the initiative and personal responsibility of the laity. See *Vida Cotidana y Santidad en la Enseñanza de San Josemaría Escrivá*, Ernest Burkhart, Javier López, (Madrid, Rialp 2012), 3rd Edition, Vol. 1, 62-66.

Seven

DEVELOPMENT OF DOCTRINE: ON RELIGIOUS TRUTHS

Catholics frequently ask, and non-Catholics even more: Will the Catholic Church change its doctrine on the second marriage of divorced Catholics, on the so-called marriage of two persons with same-sex attraction, on the ordination of women to the priesthood, and so forth? Newman provided a helpful framework to evaluate changes in doctrine that enable us to answer such contemporary questions.

The body of Catholic doctrine has grown over the centuries. New doctrines have been formulated (the Assumption of the Blessed Virgin Mary in 1950); some have been brought out more forcefully (the Church as a communion of persons); while others have been placed in their proper context (salvation within the Church vs. outside the Church).

With this in mind we could say that doctrine changes over time, but the verb "change" can be easily misunderstood. People change homes; they change professions or change their country of residence. In reference to doctrine, the verb "develop" is more precise because it connotes permanence along with growth; and a doctrine can grow and develop while remaining substantially what it was from the beginning.

Personal experience also bears evidence to the fact that, with time, our religious beliefs develop or change. We give less weight to some earlier beliefs and put aside altogether some beliefs as childish or even mistaken. We adopt new beliefs and better explanations, or we reach deeper understanding of former ones. In his search for religious truth, Newman faced the important question: Is the Roman Catholic Church the true Church founded by Jesus Christ, or is it a corruption of the original Church? It was the question of whether certain beliefs, such as prayer for the dead, the intercession of the saints, and papal authority, are true developments in doctrine or corruption of doctrine.

Newman's decision to become a Catholic depended on the answer to those questions. After studying this matter for a number of years, praying, and painstakingly weighing these thoughts, he decided that, in fact, the teachings of the Church of Rome were true developments. His *Essay on the Development of Christian Doctrine* was a record of his thoughts and discernments on this matter, which concluded with his admission to the Church of Rome on August 9, 1845.

In the essay Newman explained how human beings grasp ideas, looking at them from different angles. This process takes a long time and much effort. Doctrines are formulated gradually over time, as ideas are connected with other ideas and rightly ordered. He wrote:

> Ordinarily an idea is not brought home to the intellect as objective except through this variety; like bodily substances, which are not apprehended except under the clothing of their properties and results, and which admit of being walked round, and surveyed on opposite sides, and in different perspectives, and in contrary lights, in evidence of their reality.[1]

Ideas grow over time. "There is no one aspect deep enough to exhaust the contents of a real idea, no one term or proposition which will serve to define it. . ."[2]

As noted in an earlier chapter, the development of doctrine calls for a loving contemplation of truth. In his fifteenth *Oxford University Sermon*, Newman presented the Virgin Mary as a pattern for every believer, from the unlearned to the doctors of the Church. There he wrote,

[1] *Dev.*, 34.
[2] *Dev.*, 35.

Thus St. Mary is our pattern of Faith, both in the reception and in the study of Divine Truth. She does not think it enough to accept, she dwells upon it; not enough to possess, she uses it; not enough to assent, she develops it; not enough to submit the reason, she reasons upon it; not indeed reasoning first, and believing afterwards, with Zacharias, yet first believing without reasoning, next from love and reverence, reasoning after believing.[3]

In the *Essay on Development of Christian Doctrine*, Newman compared an idea to a spring and a river. An idea begins like a spring, but when it develops it is more like a river. He wrote:

(It) is indeed sometimes said that the stream is clearest near the spring. Whatever use may fairly be made of this image, it does not apply to the history of a philosophy or belief, which on the contrary is more equable, and purer, and stronger, when its bed has become deep, and broad, and full.[4]

What Newman had in mind was a change in continuity with the past as he noticed in the history of ecumenical councils where one council completed another; for instance, Nicea was completed by Ephesus and in our times, Vatican I by Vatican II. Ker explains this very well in reference to what he calls Newman's theology of councils.[5] He illustrates how the doctrine of infallibility put forth by Vatican I needed to be completed by the doctrine on episcopal collegiality of Vatican II, and how the hierarchical image of the Church stemming from the Council of Trent had to be completed with vision of the church fathers as the community of the baptized as elucidated in *Lumen Gentium*, the most important constitution of Vatican II. Through this development, the idea of the Church becomes a river bed that is more "deep, and broad, and full."

---

[3] John Henry Newman, *Oxford University Sermons* (London: Longmans, Green, and Co., 1909), 313.
[4] *Dev.*, 40.
[5] *Newman on Vatican II*, pp. 72-83.

Furthermore, according to Newman an idea is stimulated and expanded by trial and battles into perfection and supremacy. "From time to time it makes essays which fail, and are in consequence abandoned."[6] Thus, we arrive at the frequently quoted passage from his essay, one usually quoted, without the proper context: "In a higher world it is otherwise, but here below to live is to change, and to be perfect is to have changed often."[7]

Newman thought that change is a natural part of growth and perfection, and that, as such, development of doctrine in Christianity is to be expected. At the same time, he writes that "an infallible developing authority is to be expected," and to judge about such developments, since—due to many reasons, such as birth, education, place, personal attachment—people might interpret them differently.

The infallible voice of the Church is necessary: "Some rule is necessary for arranging and authenticating these various expressions and results of Christian doctrine."[8] This teaching authority is necessary "to impart a decision to what is vague, and confidence to what is empirical, to ratify the successive steps of so elaborate a process, and to secure the validity of inferences. . ."[9]

After speaking about this teaching authority, which rested on the pope and the bishops united to him, Newman went on to speak of seven tests or "notes" that are also helpful for ascertaining the correctness of development.[10]

Employing his terminology, the seven tests that a doctrine must pass to be accepted as a true development are the following:

1. Preservation of the type or identity (maintenance of the same characteristics);
2. Continuity of principles (maintenance of the same principles);

---

[6] *Dev.*, 40.
[7] *Dev.*, 40.
[8] *Dev.*, 77.
[9] *Dev.*, 78.
[10] Cardinal Avery Dulles explains well Newman's teaching on revelation and doctrine, and describes his seven tests for authentic development in *John Henry Newman*, (London: Continuum, 2002), 64-82.

3. Assimilative power (power of assimilation) or interpenetration of doctrines;
4. Logical consequences;
5. Anticipation of its future (foreshadowing of subsequent phases);
6. Conservative action on its past (protection of earlier phases); and
7. Chronic vigor (vigorous action from first to last).[11]

Most of the tests are a variation of the first two tests: for a doctrine to be a true development instead of a corruption, it must preserve the type and have continuity of principles with an earlier doctrine. It cannot contradict an earlier doctrine. For instance, the practice of individual confession and reconciliation preserves the spirit of conversion found in the early Church and is in continuity with Christ's forgiveness of sins in the Gospel and his instruction to the apostles to forgive men's sins. The practice of indulgences is another doctrine that does not contradict earlier doctrine. It preserves the mission of the Church and is in continuity with the doctrine of redemption and Christ's salvific will.

In light of these tests, we can briefly consider whether a proposed modern day change in doctrine regarding marriage could be accepted as a true doctrinal development. The proposed practice of allowing a married Catholic who remarried after a civil divorce to receive Holy Communion is advanced as a necessary change in doctrine based on a deeper understanding of mercy and pastoral accompaniment. This practice, however, would condone the sin of adultery and thus contradict the ageless penitential practice of abandoning a state of sin before forgiveness of the sin. Also, mercy should not be separated from justice; otherwise it would give rise to injustices to other parties. The spouse who was abandoned and did not remarry would be treated unjustly. The proposed change in the Church's discipline would not pass the first test.

[11] See *Dev.*, 171.

The tests, however, are, according to their author, "insufficient for the guidance of individuals in the case of so large and complicated a problem as Christianity though they may aid our inquiries and support our conclusions."[12] In a later chapter we will discuss further the necessary role and authority of the hierarchy in interpreting the Bible and rendering judgment on difficult moral subjects.

For contemporary society, the idea that there are definitive religious truths is something suspect and unpopular; it is "undemocratic" and goes against the widespread notion of a vague religious tolerance of all beliefs as having the same value. This attitude, a counterpart to "political correctness," could be called religious correctness. It is an exaggerated and indiscriminate tolerance of any religious belief.

There are a few possible explanations for this view: a desire to justify one's own beliefs, which may or may not be correct or true; an uncritical acceptance of religious truths; a sentimental approach to religion and the acceptance of others' beliefs; and ignorance of the Bible and Christian Tradition.

From his twenties on, Newman recognized and embraced the principle of doctrine in religion. It was among his basic tenets in religion, along with that of the immortality of the soul and the sacramentality of the visible world.[13] It is the belief in objective religious truths. An unwavering adherence to this marked his entire life to the point that, when giving an address at his conferral of the cardinal's hat, he said that his whole life's work had been to fight the spirit of "Liberalism in Religion," an error that he saw spreading over the whole world. In this address, what he said summed up what we mean today by doctrinal relativism:

> Liberalism in religion is the doctrine that there is no positive truth in religion, but that one creed is as good as another, and this is the teaching which is gaining substance and force daily. It is inconsistent with the recognition of any religion as true.

---

[12] *Dev.*, 78.

[13] This is the belief that the visible world points to the invisible world of grace, and that God communicates his graces to men through the visible world.

It teaches that all are to be tolerated, as all are matters of opinion. Revealed religion is not a truth, but a sentiment and a taste—not an objective fact, not miraculous; and it is the right of each individual to make it say just what strikes his fancy.[14]

Newman strongly criticized the practice of Evangelical Christians of his day of reducing differences in doctrine for the sake of not alienating Christians. Evangelicals only required the profession of some common doctrines, such as the belief in Christ as Savior, the need for conversion and missionary work, and the universal commandment of love. The practice of reducing religious beliefs to a few doctrines, he thought, would in the end empty Christianity of religious truths.

Today we see a similar reduction or minimization of religious truths among Catholics. Rather than giving importance to the worship of God and knowledge of revelation, religion is reduced to good works. Little by little, truths about God himself, the Church, the sacraments, and the moral life are compromised or even rejected. Religion becomes something man-made, in some cases a political program, rather man's response to God's revelation and Christ's institution of the Church.

In sum, Newman teaches that with the passage of time the Church's doctrines grow, and its teaching authority judges on the correctness of this doctrinal growth. For someone to argue that a given doctrinal change is correct, he has to demonstrate that it is, in fact, a true development, and the Magisterium must discern that this is the case. It is mistaken to assert that a change in doctrine is a true development because the times, needs, and circumstances call for this change. Yet this is precisely what some theologians do, and, seeking to lend weight to their position, they incorrectly invoke Newman's support. Often these writers miss Newman's point altogether: he wrote precisely to discriminate between authentic development and religious error.

---

[14] John Henry Newman, Biglietto Speech, May 12, 1878. Newman Reader website: http://www.newmanreader.org/works/addresses/file2.html.

Eight

BISHOPS AND POPES:
AUTHORITY IN THE CHURCH

During his life, Newman knew and dealt with many bishops, the first of which were Anglican and later, Roman Catholic. The characteristics of his relationships with them indicate the lofty idea that he had of the Church's hierarchical structure and his lifelong practice of obedience to ecclesial authority.

Newman realized that the Church instituted by Christ was organized under bishops, with the task of governing the local churches. Each bishop stands in a line of succession of bishops that dates back to the apostles. Belief in this apostolic succession is central to Anglicans and Catholics alike. The apostolic origin of the office of each bishop gives legitimacy and authority to the office. Based on its divine origin, the bishop exercises a triple office: teaching, ruling, and sanctifying. Newman gave lectures on the teaching office, which he called the prophetic office.

The Church's leadership does not consist of a democratically elected body of leaders. Instead, its leaders or pastors are appointed by the head of the Church. Newman was struck by the words of St. Cyprian, the fourth century bishop of Carthage: *nihil sine episcopo* (nothing without the bishop). Given his authority, the bishop should be obeyed in all doctrinal and disciplinary matters.

The office of ruling or governing was compromised in England, not only by the courts, but by parliament and the crown, who took upon themselves the closure of dioceses in Ireland and the establishment of a diocese in the Holy Land. There was the added offense that the latter arrangement, a joint diocese with Lutherans and Evangelicals (1841), neglected doctrinal beliefs about the nature of the Church. This was an example of the state's control of the Church for political and economic motives. The appointment of bishops was no less problematic. The committee that presented the candidates to the crown included non-Christians.

When Newman was ordained a deacon and later a clergyman in the Anglican Church, he lived a refined obedience to his bishop according to St. Cyprian's maxim. Laxity in obedience to bishops was one of the serious deficiencies that Newman and his friends sought to remedy through the Oxford Movement. The perennial problem of ecclesial discipline became more acute in nineteenth-century England: more bishops did not exercise their authority, and more clergymen disobeyed their bishops. A well-known case in point was that of a clergyman, George Cornelius Gorham, who was denied appointment to a rectory by the Bishop of Exeter on account of his unorthodox views on baptismal regeneration. The clergyman not only failed to obey the bishop's teaching office, but filed a lawsuit against the bishop. The Crown court undermined the Church's legitimate authority, deciding in favor of the clergyman.

For his part, Newman practiced obedience even in the painful and unjust decision of his bishop's call for the cessation of new *Tracts of the Times* following the publication of the controversial *Tract* 90 (1840). In the tract, Newman set out to show that the *Thirty-Nine Articles* were not opposed to the Roman Catholic Council of Trent but were a compromise between Roman Catholic and Protestant doctrinal beliefs and religious practices.[1] He politely defended his actions in writing to his bishop and man-

---

[1] Later, as a Roman Catholic, he maintained much of what he had written in *Tract* 90, except for his understanding of Transubstantiation and a section on Article XXXI which rejects the Mass as a sacrifice and the practice of a priest offering the Mass without a congregation.

aged to avoid the withdrawal of the tract, but he accepted, albeit with sadness, the bishop's request not to write any more tracts. As it was *Tract* 90 was condemned by one Anglican bishop after another. Every condemnation was a blow to Newman, who chose to remain quiet, preferring to wait and hope the storm would pass.

From the time of his youth into his middle age, Newman had been plagued by the idea that Church of Rome was the Antichrist and whore of Babylon. A long trip through the Mediterranean, and especially in Italy, had made him reconsider some of his uncritically accepted beliefs. He saw the piety of many Catholics and experienced their charity, and he visited their beautiful basilicas, especially in Rome. At that point he began to subscribe to the Branch Theory, which holds that the Catholic Church has three branches: Orthodox, Anglican, and Roman.

It was not until 1839 that he was forced to seriously examine his position regarding the Roman Catholic Church. A friend showed him an article by Nicolas Wiseman on apostolic succession in the *Dublin Review*. Wiseman argued that the Anglican Church was schismatic and thus could not claim apostolic succession. Wiseman quoted St. Augustine who, disputing the Donatist heresy, had written: "Wherefore the entire world judges with security that they are not good who separate themselves from the entire world."[2] A historical analysis of the role of the papacy led Newman to change his previous beliefs. Newman recognized that in the fourth and fifth centuries, Christians looked to Rome to settle doctrinal and disciplinary disputes. The See of St. Peter exercised an authority granted to the apostle Peter and his successors by Christ himself.

In 1841 a number of the factors adduced earlier, along with his study of the Arian heresy, combined to shatter his faith in the Anglican Church. He finally broke his silence from the pulpit of St. Mary, the Oxford University Church; and on four consecutive

---

[2] St. Augustine, *Cont. Epist. Parmen. Lib. Iii, cap 3*. Quoted by Nicholas Wiseman in "The Anglican Claim of Apostolical Succession" in *Dublin Review*, 1839, quoted from London, *Publications of the Catholic Truth Society*, Vol. XXIV, 1895, 23.

Sundays, he preached his Samaritan Sermons on the notes of the Church: antiquity, apostolic succession, Catholicity and holiness. He spoke of the invisible presence of God in the Church. He no longer defended the Anglican Church but invited the congregation to trust in God's providence and remain where each one had been placed by God.

Newman's conversion to Roman Catholicism was thus tied to a new understanding of both papal and episcopal authority and apostolic succession. He knew too much about history to think that popes and bishops did not err or fall into personal sins. He believed, however, that the Holy Spirit guides the Church, keeping its chief pastor and the body of the bishops as a whole from erring in matters of faith and morals.

Nicholas Wiseman, the Catholic Bishop for the Central District of England, and Newman had known each other in Rome, when the former was the head of the English College there. Wiseman anxiously waited for Newman's reception into the Church, and when this took place, he advised him to live with his fellow converts at Oscott College and to soon afterwards pursue theological studies in Rome and ordination to the priesthood. Until then, their relationship was good, but that gradually changed for the worse, especially due to William Faber's influence on Wiseman.

Faber, himself a convert, had formed a community of men and wished to join with Newman, something that Wiseman advised Newman to accept. Against his wishes and better judgment, Newman accepted Faber and his companions. Faber soon became a thorn in Newman's side by wishing to impose Italian customs on English Catholics and being overzealous in his apostolate. Worst of all Faber, who became a confidant of Wiseman, poisoned Newman's relationship with Wiseman, who was by then the Bishop of Westminster, the Catholic diocese for London.

Newman's Relationship with the Irish Bishops

Only a few years after ordination to the priesthood, Newman was faced with dealing on a personal basis with the Irish bishops, under whose care rested the Catholic University of Ireland, which was established with Newman as its first rector (1854).[3] Ireland faced in this period great economic hardship, and there was a strong dislike toward anything English. One of the university's most important difficulties was finding students and teachers. Wealthy families preferred to send their sons to Queens College in Dublin. Some of the Irish bishops were opposed to having as rector an Englishman and, as teachers, Newman's convert friends. Despite these difficulties, Newman traveled throughout Ireland visiting with each prelate, and through his efforts he was successful in obtaining contributions from most of the dioceses for a collection for the university.

Paul Cullen, Archbishop of Armagh, and later of Dublin, was the driving force for the establishment of the University of Ireland, and he sought Newman as its first rector. Unfortunately, he did not work well with Newman, and, although the University got off to a good start, its enrollment did not grow and its financial struggles only increased.

Initially, Cullen thought that having Newman appointed bishop would give the English priest a better standing as rector and in his relations with the university's board of Irish bishops. Cullen proposed this to the Holy See, but when the nomination seemed imminent, he changed his mind and advised against it. The rumor of his nomination and its reversal was embarrassing for Newman, and his difficulties with Cullen increased. The archbishop did not fully trust the university rector and had unrealistic expectations, but most of all he did not understand and appreciate Newman's idea of an educated laity and their role at the university and in society at large.

Despite these misunderstandings, Newman did have friends who were bishops, archbishops and cardinals, including David Moriarity, an Irish bishop who appreciated his work in Ireland.[4]

---

[3] This is the subject of chapter X of this book.

[4] In a preface to Newman's posthumous volume *Meditations and Devotions*, in addition to Bishop James O'Connor, Fr. William Neville lists the following: Cardinal Alimonda, Archbishop of Turin; Cardinal Place, Archbishop of Rennes; Cardinal Macchi; Cardinal Capecelatro, Archbishop of Capua; and Msgr. Stonor, Archbishop of Trebizond.

Another of Newman's friends was James O'Connor, Bishop of Omaha, with whom Newman had forged a friendship when studying at the College for Propaganda Fidei. It was friendship that lasted the whole of Newman's life as a Catholic.

Papal Infallibility

In 1870, the First Vatican Council was held in Rome, and one of the principal subjects addressed was the pope's authority; the other was revelation. Newman was invited as a theological consultant by various bishops and even by Pius XI. He declined, arguing that he was not a theologian, but closely followed the discussions that led to the declaration of the dogma of papal infallibility. Newman was concerned with ultramontanists—such as W. G. Ward, who wished to increase the scope of papal teaching binding in conscience—and with the timing of this declaration for the Church in England, which faced a lot of suspicion and antagonism from Anglicans. He joked that Ward would like a papal bull served with breakfast every morning.

Newman did not openly oppose the declaration of this dogma, and when Pope Pius XI announced it, Newman embraced and defended it. The reaction in England against the bull was as expected. William Gladstone, the English Prime Minister, publicly criticized the council decrees, arguing that it would lead men to relinquish their moral and intellectual freedom and to abandon their civil responsibilities on the basis of a foreign authority.

Newman responded with an open letter to the Duke of Norfolk. This now-famous essay explained the purpose and limits of papal infallibility. He noted that,

> [the pope] speaks *ex cathedrâ*, or infallibly, when he speaks, first, as the Universal Teacher; secondly, in the name and with the authority of the Apostles; thirdly, on a point of faith or morals; fourthly, with the purpose of binding every member of the Church to accept and believe his decision.[5]

[5] *Letter to the Duke of Norfolk in Diff.*, Vol. 2, 325.

Thus the pope does not speak infallibly when giving his opinion in interpreting the Scriptures or the church fathers and much less on scientific matters. In moral subjects, his definition must be circumscribed to matters of the moral law contained in the Scriptures and matters necessary for salvation that apply to all men.

Given these restrictions and, in particular, the fact that infallibility does not apply to orders directed to particular countries or political or religious classes, he asserted that there was no opposition between being a loyal English citizen and a faithful Roman Catholic. It was in this essay, as discussed earlier, in which this English writer masterfully expounded on the role of the moral conscience.

During his life Newman had connections to three popes: Gregory XVI, Pius XI, and Leo XIII. The first one, Pope Gregory, he did not meet, but upon Newman's admission to the Roman Catholic Church, this pope sent him an apostolic blessing and the gift of a silver crucifix with a relic of the true cross. The date on the certificate of the sacred relic coincided with the same day *Tract* 90 had been published.

Newman understood the difficult historical circumstances faced by the Church and especially by its head. He wrote:

> The Popes have been, and are, of course Conservatives in the right sense of the word; that is, they cannot bear anarchy, think revolution an evil, they pray for the peace of the world (. . .) and they effectively support the cause of order and good government. . ."[6]

Newman did not think the pope was a conservative in the political sense, for the sake of power or external forms. He wrote that some saintly bishops and great pontiffs were detached from everything and ready to sell Church property to relieve hunger or to redeem captives. Although they had been old men, "popes have never found any difficulty, when the proper moment came, of fol-

[6] John Henry Newman, "The Rise and Progress of Universities" in *Historical Sketches*, Vol. 3 [1872] (London: Longmans, Green, and Co., 1909),: 131-134. From here on *HS*.

lowing out a new and daring line of policy."[7] He gave as an example the bold initiatives of reform of the administration of the Papal States by Pope Gregory, "a man of eighty, of humble origin, the most conservative of popes, as he was considered."[8] Commenting on this, Ian Ker writes that the modern reader can hardly help but think of Pope John XXIII, an aged pope, of poor family, who called the Second Vatican Council.[9]

The new convert was the object of kindness and respect from the popes. When he went to Rome for studies in theology, Pope Pius XI summoned him and greeted him cordially. At the first meeting, Newman hit the pope's knee with his head as he bent down to kiss his foot. The same pope would offer Newman a magnificent house of the Oratory on the island of Malta as the future novitiate house, but this did not materialize. After his ordination to the priesthood on May 30, 1847, he began his Oratorian novitiate at Santa Croce in Rome, with other members of his Maryvale community. There he received the Papal Brief making him Superior of the English Oratory.

Leo XIII succeeded Pius XI in 1878, and Newman was very pleased to hear of the new pontiff's intention of working for the reconciliation between the Church and the modern world. At Christmas he received a signed holy picture from the pope's breviary, sent by one of Newman's penitents who was then a governess in Rome. It was a token of what was to follow. In January 1879, the Papal Secretary of State wrote Cardinal Manning, asking him to find out how Newman would respond to the invitation to become a cardinal. The Duke of Norfolk had written the pope to make this suggestion, but it seems that it was already the intention of the pope, who when he was the papal nuncio in Brussels, had heard of the Oxford Movement and in 1845 met with Fr. Barberi immediately after he had received Newman into the Church.

[7] *HS*, 131–134.
[8] Ian Ker, *John Henry Newman* (Oxford University Press, 1988), 411.
[9] Ker, *John Henry Newman*, 411.

Cardinal Manning informed Newman through Ullathorne, the Bishop of Birmingham. Newman told Ullathorne that he did not wish to reside in Rome, which was the custom for cardinals who were not diocesan bishops. He did not refuse the honor proffered to him, but Cardinal Manning, who was Archbishop of London, sent to Rome a letter from Newman stating his concern, without adding an explanatory letter from Bishop Ullathorne.[10]

When a rumor in London, followed by a report in the *Times*, claimed that Newman had refused appointment as cardinal, Bishop Ullathorne wrote directly to the Secretary of State to explain Newman's gratitude and wish to accept the Pope's invitation. In the end, Cardinal Manning was obliged to explain to the pope Newman's desire to remain in England, and the pope consequently waived the requirement of residence in Rome.

This papal act bore great significance both for Newman and England. Upon hearing the news, Newman wrote:

> It puts an end to all those reports that my teaching is not Catholic or my books trustworthy, which have been so great a trial to me so long. (To have refused the honor) would have created a suspicion that it was true that I was but half and half Catholic, who dared not commit himself to a close union with the Church of Rome, and who wished to be independent.[11]

Newman had other reasons to accept the honor. He did not wish to upset Catholics, deter potential converts, or dishearten friends who wished that his name be vindicated. He explained to an Anglican friend, R. W. Church—who might have been surprised that he would accept this ecclesiastical position—that he would not dare refuse the offer:

> A good Providence gave me an opportunity of clearing myself of former calumnies in my Apologia—and I dared not refuse it—And now He gave me the means (. . .) to set myself right

---

[10] See Ker's *John Henry Newman* for a detailed account of the affair, 214-222.
[11] JHN to Anne Mozley (March 1, 1879) in *LD*, Vol. 29, 50.

as regards other calumnies that were directed against me—
how could I neglect so great a loving kindness?[12]

Years later Pope Leo XIII told an English visitor about the appointment:

> My Cardinal! it was not easy, it was not easy. They say he was
> too liberal, but I had determined to honour the Church in
> honouring Newman, I always had a cult for him. I am proud
> that I was able to honour such a man.[13]

Other popes would later have important things to say about Cardinal Newman. In 1908, Pius X replied to a letter by the Bishop of Limerick affirming Newman's orthodoxy. In 1998, John Paul II referenced Newman in his encyclical letter *Fides et ratio* and later named him Servant of God. Most recently on September 20, 2010, Benedict XVI beatified him.

As noted in this chapter, according to Newman the Church's hierarchy fulfills a divine mission and, within its scope in matters of faith and morals, the hierarchy is protected from error by the Holy Spirit. But bishops and popes are mere men and subject to misunderstandings, envy, and other faults. Although the Bishop of Birmingham and, later, Pope Leo XIII, praised Newman, he often had to wrestle with accepting injustice from the hierarchy, and at times had to retreat, wishing to be left alone. It was through prayer that he was able to suffer and persevere during periods of sadness and disappointment. To those bishops who treated him unjustly he responded with charity. To the popes who dealt with him kindly and vindicated his orthodoxy he was forever grateful.

---

[12] JHN to R.W. Church (March 11, 1879) in *LD*, Vol. 29: 72.
[13] Lady Sophia Palmer to Lady Laura Ridding in *Sophia Matilda Palmer de Franqueville, 1852-1915, a Memoir*, quoted in LD, Vol. 29: 426.

Nine

CELIBACY AND MARRIAGE

As Ian Ker has rightly pointed out, a very important doctrine of *Lumen Gentium*, contained in chapters 1 and 2, is the renewed description of the Church in biblical and patristic terms; the Church is the people of God, the body of Christ, and the community of the baptized. Newman would have rejoiced to see this ecclesiology since he did not consider the Church divided into hierarchy, clergy, and laity as has been emphasized after the reading of the subsequent chapters of *Lumen Gentium*.[1] For him the Church is the community of the baptized through the action of the Holy Spirit in the sacraments.

The Church has a charismatic dimension in which the members have different gifts (*charisms*) and vocations. From the start its members included both celibate and married men and women. Newman did not write much about celibacy and marriage, both of which are a calling from God. In the nineteenth century, marriage, as the natural and permanent bond between man and woman established by God and sanctioned by the Church, was generally unquestioned. When he referred to either state in life, it was to emphasize that it is a divine vocation. Newman, as we will see, felt called to dedicate himself exclusively to God's service by remaining a celibate man.

Newman experienced a good and happy family life as a young boy. There is no explicit account of his parents' relationship, but he did recall the happiness of his childhood and close relations with his paternal grandmother and aunt Elizabeth.

[1] *Newman on Vatican II*, 84-106.

During Newman's childhood, his father suffered various financial downfalls, which affected the family's living conditions and produced serious concern, especially for the parents. Mr. Newman continued, however, to support the education of his eldest son whom he had enrolled at Trinity College, Oxford. They were proud of his academic achievements and congratulated him.

Newman's experience of his parents' marriage and the family life was thus a healthy one without any significant regrets and sadness except for the financial collapse of the family's livelihood. His family and those of his close friends were a sound reference point in his universe. The roles of father and mother, as well as children and other extended family members, were clear and important. Respect and affection, support and obedience were a natural part of family life.

Family letters to him convey the sense of a peaceful domestic life and later, the shock and sadness of the premature death of his father, most likely affected by the financial pressures he faced. Newman traveled to London for his funeral, and assumed the role as the head of the family.

Well before his death, Mr. Newman had manifested the desire for his son to study law, which Newman had entertained by enrolling at Lincoln's Inn in November of 1819. The following year he overworked himself, at one point studying thirteen to fourteen hours a day, to prepare for his final exams. He was overwhelmed and did not do well, although he obtained his degree. In this blow to his pride, Newman realized that he had been aiming at the wrong objective, and in a letter to his spiritual mentor Walter Mayers he confided: "I think I see clearly that honour and fame are not desirable. God is leading me through life in the way best adapted for His glory and my own salvation."[2]

In 1821, Newman returned to Oxford, where he had a scholarship for nine years, and began to give private tutoring lessons. That year his father told him he must make up his mind what he wanted to do in life. Newman made the decision to enter into the

---

[2] JHN to Walter Mayers, (January 1821), *LD*, Vol. 1: 99.

Church, a decision his father accepted in view of his son's pronounced religious inclination.

He continued at Oxford and was elected a fellow at Oriel College in April 1822. Mayers advised him to take orders, and on June 13, 1824, Newman was ordained a deacon in Christ Church Cathedral. He wrote in his diary:

> It is over. I am thine, O Lord; I seem quite dizzy, and cannot altogether believe and understand it. At first, after the hands were laid on me, my heart shuddered within me; the words "forever" are so terrible.[3]

His sincere evangelical fervor strengthened his sense of purpose, and he threw himself into pastoral care as a curate for the working-class parish of St. Clement on the outskirts of Oxford. He felt awkward among poor and ignorant people, but he applied himself willingly; within ten days he had visited a third of his parishioners, and by the middle of August, he had gone to every home in the parish. He preached at Sunday services, challenging the attendants to a stricter observance of Christian life. When he heard that some thought him to be too demanding, he replied:

> Those who make comfort the great subject of their preaching seem to mistake the end of their ministry. *Holiness* is the great end. There must be a struggle and a trial here. Comfort is a cordial, but no one drinks cordials from morning to night.[4]

He also visited the sick to pray with them and offer some comfort. They were moved by his visits and expressed their gratefulness.

At the same time he was curate at St. Clement's, he took on the role of dean, bursar and tutor at St. Alban's Hall. Then a year after becoming deacon, on May 29, 1825, Newman was ordained an Anglican priest. The following year he was made a tutor at Oriel and was obliged to leave his work as curate.

---

[3] John Henry Newman, *Autobiographical Writings*, (New York: Sheed and Ward, 1957), 200. From here on *AW*.
[4] *AW*, 172.

In 1828, Newman became rector of St. Mary the Virgin, the university parish, when Edward Hawkins, who was rector, left to become provost of Oriel College. St. Mary would be the place where, over the course of a dozen years, Newman delivered memorable sermons as well as lectures.

Anglican clergymen often married and lived with their families in a parish rectory, but there was a tradition at Oxford of clergymen who remained celibate and dedicated themselves to the spiritual care and teaching of the undergraduates. In Newman's time at Oxford that tradition changed significantly. The office of fellows, traditionally held by men who remained celibate, was then also held by married men. Some of Newman's friends, such as Dr. Ogle and Edward B. Pusey who taught at Oxford, were married men. Others such as John Keble and Richard Whately vacated their fellowship before or after marrying.

His Anglican friend Hurrell Froude helped him to appreciate the ideal of celibacy. Froude spoke of the intrinsic excellence of virginity and considered the Blessed Virgin Mary as its greatest pattern.[5] Newman thought the country parsons ought to marry as a rule but that "there should be among the clergy enough unmarried to give a character of strength to the whole."[6] With the start of the Oxford Movement, he saw more clearly the need for a celibate clergy that would dedicate itself exclusively to the spiritual renewal and care of the Church. He envisioned celibate clergymen, not only at Oxford but also in the large cities, exercising their priestly work and educating the poor.

Being of this mindset, he was surprised when his good friend Henry Wilberforce, a member of the Oxford Movement, told him of his plans to marry. Newman was upset, in part because he thought that his friend had kept the plans from him but even more because of the lessening of their friendship this would entail. For his part, Wilberforce seems to have worried about telling his friend of his plans precisely because of Newman's views about the

[5] See *Apo.*, 34.
[6] JHN to Henry Wilberforce, (February 26, 1832), *LD*, Vol. 3: 23.

importance of celibate clergymen for the Oxford Movement. In any event, Newman and Henry Wilberforce remained close friends all their lives.

Priestly celibacy dates back to early Christianity as far back as the second century—even though it was only mandated at the beginning of the fourth century in Spain and many centuries later for the entire West. In the eastern part of the Roman Empire, priests either remained celibate, living in monastic communities, or married prior to ordination to the priesthood. Only celibate priests were chosen for the episcopate.

As a clergyman in the Anglican Church, Newman was not obliged to remain celibate. He chose freely to do so and never seemed to have had any interest in pursuing marriage. He saw the need for a complete dedication to the priesthood, which would preclude marriage. In a letter he mentioned the family comforts that marriage would provide; and he was aware that he would be giving up the companionship of a wife and her care of the home. When his father died, a few months after his ordination as deacon, he wrote: "My mother said the other day she hoped to live to see me married, but I think *I* shall either die within a College walls, or a Missionary in a foreign land—no matter where, so I die in Christ."[7]

Many years later, once a Roman Catholic, Newman criticized the romantic view of married priesthood that presented marriage as a safeguard to the priestly vocation. He explained that the experience of married clergymen indicates that marriage does not make them necessarily more virtuous and, in particular, chaste. "I am very sceptical indeed that in matter of fact a married clergy *is* adorned, in any special and singular way, with the grace of purity; and that is just the very thing which Protestants take for granted."[8]

[7] *AW*, 203.
[8] John Henry Newman, *Lectures on the Present Position of Catholics in England*, [1851],(London: Longmans, Green, and Co., 1908), 134. From here on *Pres. Pos.*

Further, he felt that chastity is a gift from God, which requires sacrifice and prayer for the celibate as well as the married man; that chastity moderates the sexual desire; and that a person who does not practice this virtue will not be chaste by the very fact of his being married. Thus he repeated his point in a stronger manner. In the case of a Protestant rector or dissenting clergyman who happened to be married:

> (. . .) when he offends, whether in a grave way or less seriously, still in all cases he has by matrimony but exchanged a bad sin for a worse, and has become an adulterer instead of being a seducer. Matrimony only does this for him, that his purity is at once less protected and less suspected.[9]

Newman understood the priesthood as a sacred order at the service of the faithful. The priest serves men and women by blessing their marriage, baptizing their children, and teaching them the truths of the Faith.

Christian Marriage

Even though marriage *per se* was not questioned at large in the nineteenth century, ignorance existed about its sacramental nature. Christians believe that Baptism is the door to the other sacraments and that it is by virtue of that bond with Christ that a man and a woman are united to Christ in Christian marriage.

While still a very young Anglican clergyman, Newman faced the situation of a young woman in his parish who was unbaptized yet wished to wed in a Christian marriage. He offered to baptize her first and, when she did not accept, refused to officiate her marriage. The woman finally went to a dissenting clergyman to be married while Newman, who acted to uphold Church doctrine, was unjustly reprimanded by his bishop.

Years later, Newman often wrote on subjects when the occasion arose and usually when there was controversy about an important

---

[9] *Pres. Pos.*, 134-135.

issue. In this case, however, being a young clergyman having been corrected by the bishop, he did not write on the matter. Neither did he preach nor write on the subject of marriage itself, but in his sermons he spoke of the virtues necessary for Christian spouses; and from his friendships with married couples, we can see his great respect for the institution of marriage.

In the home of his close friend William Bowden, Newman saw a good example of a Christian family. He enjoyed visiting the Bowden residence when he went to London for business, and he was part of some of the important moments in the life of the family. After William's early death, his wife Elizabeth and some of her children would become Roman Catholics.

Another exemplary family to which he was very attached was that of Edward B. Pusey. Newman was a welcome guest to the Pusey family home at Oxford. He comforted Mrs. Pusey in her poor health and later at the time of her death. He did the same with their daughter, who was very fond of Newman and died at a young age.

Two of his students, Thomas and John Mozley, married his sisters, Harriet and Jemima, respectively. Newman was a good brother-in-law to them, and although over the years their paths parted over religious differences, he remained in contact with his sisters and their children. His sister-in-law, Anne Mozley, edited his Anglican papers.

What he had lived in his own family and seen in the families of his friends he applied in his dealings with children. In 1840, he began a Sunday school for the children at Littlemore, a village just outside Oxford. Like a good father, he was concerned for their dress, religious instruction, and singing. Many years later, he would care with similar concern for the boys at the Oratory School in Birmingham, with the aid of some of women.

Religious life

Religious life for men or women is another important Christian vocation. Religious houses have made lasting contributions to the

Church and society as centers of spirituality, education, and social assistance. As an Anglican, Newman warned that unless the Church of England allowed expressions of devotion and spirituality such as monasteries, there would be continual defections to Rome. His desire for this materialized in 1842 when he began a quasi-monastic community at Littlemore.

Newman discussed with Pusey the revival of the tradition of celibate women living in communities. He was a spiritual director for some women who became Roman Catholic and who afterwards embraced a celibate life in religious communities. Two of them, Maria Giberne, and Marianne Bowden, became nuns of the Visitation Order and maintained an ongoing and frequent correspondence with Newman.

His appreciation for communities of celibate men and women, in the monastic tradition, is evident in his writings on the Benedictine Order in *Historical Sketches*. As an Anglican, he had read St. Athanasius' *Life of St. Anthony*, the founder of western monasticism, and had written some articles about it titled "Church of the Fathers."

Responding to the claims of a former fellow of Oriel that monks had been exalted in the Middle Ages, Newman argued that monks were the set of men nearest to Christian perfection, who dedicated themselves to prayer and penance for the sake of the world, interceding to God on its behalf.

Once a Roman Catholic, Newman considered becoming a member of a religious community, and he looked to the foundations of three great founders whom he admired: St. Benedict, St. Dominic and St. Ignatius. He valued the charismatic mission of these saints in the history of the Church. St. Benedict had preserved the principle of civilization and learning in society; St. Dominic had brought on another ecclesiastical revolution with the study and teaching of the Faith; and lastly, the Jesuits and other religious communities offered still another revolution in teaching and in the missions.

Finally, after much discernment, Newman joined not a religious order but the Oratory of St. Philip Neri. In the sixteenth century,

St. Philip had been successively influenced by the three saints
mentioned above, and Newman preferred Philip's appreciation
for literature and art, poetry and history, painting and music,
which he taught others to sanctify in ordinary life. According to
Newman, the spirit of St. Philip was "to conceal seriousness under
great cheerfulness, simplicity, modesty, and humor."[10] Writing to
someone who was studying theology at St. Sulpice and was considering joining the Oratory, Newman explained:

> The discipline of the Sulpicians is much more like the Jesuits
> —it might perhaps make a Jesuit, but would not make an
> Oratorian. Do not suspect me of undervaluing the Jesuits—
> I have a profound admiration for them—but we are not Jesu-
> its.[11]

With his characteristic reference to the classics, Newman invoked
the comparison between the Athenians and Spartans in Pericles'
Funeral Oration:

> We are Athenians, the Jesuits Spartans. Ours is in one respect
> more anxious and difficult—we have no vows, we have fewer
> rules—yet we must keep together—we require knowledge of
> each other which the Jesuits do not require.[12]

Thus, with appreciation for the great variety of ways to live the
faith, Newman underlined the vocational dimension common to
each Christian: the calling is unique and respects each person's
temperament and circumstances. Each person is called by God to
a particular task and, in this consists a person's happiness:

> God knows what is my greatest happiness, but I do not. There
> is no rule about what is happy and good; what suits one
> would not suit another. And the ways by which perfection is
> reached vary very much (. . .) Thus God leads us by strange

[10] JHN to T. F. Knox, *LD*, Vol 12, Sept. 10, 1847, 113.
[11] JHN to T. F. Knox, *LD*, Vol 12,: 113.
[12] JHN to T. F. Knox, *LD*, Vol 12,: 113.

ways (. . .) We are blind; left to ourselves we should take the wrong way; we must leave it to Him.[13]

For Newman, each person must discern the path that God has marked out for him, either in celibacy or marriage, and serve his Creator there, aspiring to holiness in the fulfillment of his duties.

[13] *MD*, 299-300.

Ten

THE CHRISTIAN GENTLEMAN

In Discourse 8 of *The Idea of a University*, Newman penned an elegant and attractive description of a refined or cultured man. In time, many have come to regard this as Newman's definition of an ideal gentleman. It must be stated at the outset, however, that this assumption is an error due to a misreading of Newman's text, and in reality does not portray Newman's "ideal gentleman"—all of which will be discussed further here.

Rather than a definition, Newman gave a very long description of the qualities of a gentleman praised by men.[1] Some of the lines read as follows:

> He has his eyes on all his company; he is tender towards the bashful, gentle towards the distant, and merciful towards the absurd; he can recollect to whom he is speaking; he guards against unseasonable allusions, or topics which may irritate; he is seldom prominent in conversation, and never wearisome. He makes light of favours while he does them, and seems to be receiving when he is conferring. He never speaks of himself except when compelled, never defends himself by a mere retort, he has no ears for slander or gossip, is scrupulous in imputing motives to those who interfere with him, and interprets every thing for the best.[2]

At first glance it seems difficult to find fault with the description because it includes genuine virtue. However, throughout his dis-

---

[1] The entire description is transcribed at the end of this chapter.
[2] John Henry Newman, *The Idea of a University*, [1873] (London: Longmans, Green, and Co., 1907), 209. From here on *Idea*.

course, Newman rebutted the ideas of the English historian, Edward Gibbon (1737-1794), and social reformer and philanthropist, Lord Shaftesbury (1671-1713), who thought that man can reach perfection without religion; and they went on further to assert that men are harmed by the Christian religion.[3] Newman discussed the difference between nature and grace, and how grace builds on nature. Gibbon and Shaftesbury were content with a man without religion; for them nature was sufficient to itself—man has no need for redemption.

Newman explained how knowledge has a natural tendency to refine the mind, making it recoil from excesses and the enormity of evil. This trait was portrayed in Henryk Sienkiewicz's novel *Quo Vadis* by Patronius, the uncle of Vinicius, the protagonist. Although not a Christian, Patronius abhorred cruelty and injustice toward Christians.

Newman explained that reason and the tastes it forms:

> (. . .) generate within the mind a fastidiousness, analogous to the delicacy or daintiness which good nurture or sickly habit induces in respect of food; and this fastidiousness, though arguing no high principle, though no protection in the case of violent temptation, nor sure in its operation, yet will often or generally be lively enough to create a loathing of certain offences, or a detestation and scorn of them as ungentlemanlike (. . .)[4]

Gibbon and others did not recognize or admit that society, as they knew it, lived on the inheritance of eighteen centuries of Christianity where the ideals of truthfulness, moderation, chastity, and other virtues had superseded the Roman virtues and become enshrined in the culture's conscience.

---

[3] Anthony Ashley Cooper, 3rd Earl of Shaftesbury, was a Christian, yet his philosophical views were closer to deism. He doubted Christian belief in miracles and the authority of the Bible. "Shaftesbury was a proponent of natural religion. He denied that humans need supernatural revelation in order to discover and realize what constitutes true religion. Shaftesbury's natural religion had much in common with the views of the English Deists." Stanford Encyclopedia of Philosophy, http://plato.stanford.edu/entries/shaftesbury/#8.
[4] *Idea*, 187.

Newman also pointed out that the natural sense of shame can act as an obstacle to wrongful behavior and that remorse of evils committed can prevent future excesses. He noted that libraries, scientific lectures, museums, gardens, and other things that please the eye and give repose to feelings can exert a positive influence on our moral nature. This mental refinement is, however, very different from genuine religion.

The moral conscience, which inflicts fear and shame that should lead us to God, becomes instead a source of feelings of self-reproach:

> Fear implies the transgression of a law, and a law implies a lawgiver and judge; but the tendency of intellectual culture is to swallow up the fear in the self-reproach, and self-reproach is directed and limited to our mere sense of what is fitting and becoming (. . .) conscience tends to become what is called a moral sense; the command of duty is a sort of taste; sin is not an offense against God, but against human nature.[5]

The moral order is overturned although not in appearance. The center of the universe becomes man and God is overthrown. Only what offends man is considered a sin. Those who think in this manner have a mistaken self-centered notion of conscience:

> (. . .) it is because conscience to them is not the word of a lawgiver, as it ought to be, but the dictate of their own minds and nothing more; it is because they do not look through and beyond their own minds to their Maker, but are engrossed in notions of what is due to themselves, to their own dignity and their own consistency. Their conscience has become mere self-respect.[6]

This so-called gentleman does not feel contrition when he does wrong—only remorse and sense of degradation—and he does not seek forgiveness in the Sacrament of Confession. The result is the substitution of conscience for a moral sense or taste.

[5] *Idea*, 191.
[6] *Idea*, 192.

In this flat way of seeing life—just on a natural plane, excluding the supernatural—virtue is nothing more than being graceful in words and actions. Newman was quite clear in stating that "a philosopher's, a gentleman's religion, is of a liberal and generous character; it is based on honour; vice is evil, because it is unworthy, despicable and odious."[7] It is not the philosopher's fault; a natural plane alone is insufficient.

Newman noted that the ancient heathen quarreled with Christianity because, instead of fixing its mind on the fair and pleasant, it included a consideration of man's "sad and painful nature" and spoke of suffering and of the Cross, as well as of purgatory and hell. We can imagine Gibbon's criticism of the early Christians written in the nineteenth century.

The figure of the pagan gentleman is illustrated by Newman with a portrait of Emperor Julian, a Christian apostate and foe of Christian education. After describing his noble moral deportment, frugality, austerity, military valor, knowledge of literature, and other accomplishments, Newman reported Julian's parting words on his own deathbed. These were words of serene and proud self-sufficiency. And he commented:

Such (. . .) is the final exhibition of the Religion of Reason: in the insensibility of conscience, in the ignorance of the very idea of sin, in the contemplation of his own moral consistency, in the simple absence of fear, in the cloudless self-confidence, in the serene self-possession, in the cold self-satisfaction, we recognize the mere Philosopher.[8]

Like Gibbon, Lord Shaftesbury attacked Christianity for its doctrine of reward and punishment. The latter mocked the Christian's virtue: "There is not more of rectitude, piety or sanctity, in a creature thus reformed, than there is meekness or gentleness in a tiger strongly chained, or innocence and sobriety in a monkey under the discipline of a whip."[9] This servile obedience should be

[7] *Idea*, 193.
[8] *Idea*, 195-196.
[9] Lord Shaftesbury. Characteristics of *Men, Manners, Opinions and Times* (1732), quoted in *Idea*, 197.

criticized, but Shaftesbury's wholesale characterization of the Christian was unjust and condescending. Newman concluded that, according to Lord Shaftesbury, "Christianity is the enemy of moral virtue, as influencing the mind by fear of God, not by love of God."[10] The attack, repeated by Nietzsche, could not fathom true virtue and higher motives.

Although all men should cultivate virtue and perfect their human nature, a Christian understands that virtue is both natural and supernatural. It is not acquired through reason alone nor through human effort. Whereas Shaftesbury pursued natural beauty, making it synonymous with truth, the Christian seeks what is good, which is also beautiful and true. For Shaftesbury, Newman explained, "virtue being only one kind of beauty, the principle which determines what is virtuous is, not conscience, but *taste*."

It is plain thus that, for men who ignore the supernatural and religion, good taste in words and speech, dress and the arts, etc., will define the world's ideal of a gentleman. Beauty elicits admiration and is considered the measure of virtue. Deformity and vulgarity are vices and inspire derision. Newman criticizes this superficial view of things. He goes further, indicating another error in this way of thinking: "It is detection, not the sin, which is the crime; private life is sacred, and inquiry into it is intolerable; and decency is virtue. . . ."

This type of morality contrasts with a Christian morality, which looks to the interior of man, his desires and intentions, and offers him a real possibility of interior regeneration and not an external appearance of beauty. It aims at "regenerating the very depths of the heart."[11] St. Paul teaches the importance of charity in men's dealings with others. The Christian should be kind, patient, meek and humble. He should be calm and cheerful and act with justice, courtesy, and gentleness toward others. But to help a Christian to live in this way, the Church begins with what is essential: living in

[10] *Idea*, 197.
[11] *Idea*, 203.

1. Newman family sketch by Maria Giberne, ca 1830. *Left to right:* Francis, Mrs. Newman, Harriet, John Henry, Jemima

2. Trinity College, Oxford. Newman was an undergraduate and a scholar at Trinity from 1817–1821

3. Quad at Oriel College, Oxford. Newman was a Fellow at Oriel College from 1822–1845

4. University Church of
St. Mary the Virgin, Oxford.
Newman was the Vicar from
1828–1843

5. The pulpit of St. Mary
the Virgin. Many students
and tutors went to hear
Newman's Sunday sermons

6. Church of St. Mary the Virgin and St. Nicholas in Littlemore.
The church, built by Newman, was consecrated in 1836

7. Engraving of Newman
by Henry MacLean,
based on a portrait by
George Richmond, 1845

8. Newman's desk at Littlemore. Newman used it to write *The Development of Christian Doctrine*

9. University House at 87 St. Stephen's Green, Dublin. To the right is the entrance of the University Church Our Lady Seat of Wisdom. Newman was first rector of the Catholic University of Ireland

10. Interior of the University Church Our Lady Seat of Wisdom, Dublin. Newman had this church built in 1856

11. Newman's writing desk in his room at the Birmingham Oratory from 1851–1890

12. Fr. Newman, wearing a cassock and a biretta, ca 1866

13. Photograph of Cardinal Newman by Louis Barraud (1885). Pope Leo XIII made Newman a cardinal in 1879

14. Cardinal Newman Library at the Birmingham Oratory. Newman moved there in 1851 and brought with him many of the books today in the library

15. Cardinal Newman's private Chapel at the Birmingham Oratory

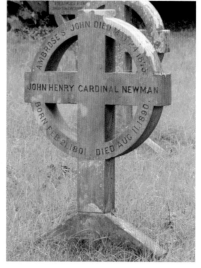

16. Newman's tombstone at Rednal, outside Birmingham. In 2010 his remains were exhumed and taken to the Birmingham Oratory

a state of grace, and practicing the virtues of faith, hope, charity and piety. This vision of a Christian morality corrects the notion of a "gentleman," which, according to Newman, is a creation of civilization and not of Christianity.

To be more precise, Newman specifically indicated that man is in need of salvation; he is sinful and needs to overcome sin, especially pride and vanity. Rather than humility, the world encourages modesty, which is only a counterfeit. "This is how it can be proud at the very time that it is unassuming."[12] The proud man is condescending toward others, acting their superior. In this way, pride acquires the new name of "self-respect," and "delicacy and gentleness are its attire, and good sense and sense of honour direct its motions."[13]

According to Newman pride has become "the very staple of the religion and morality"[14] of his time. He next describes how this pride is manifest in the varied occupations of life:

> It becomes the safeguard of chastity, the guarantee of veracity, in high and low it is the very household god of society, as at present constituted, inspiring neatness and decency in the servant girl, propriety of carriage, and refined manners in her mistress, uprightness, manliness, and generosity in the head of the family. It diffuses a light over town and country; it covers the soil with handsome edifices and smiling gardens; it tills the field, it stocks and embellishes the shop. It is the stimulating principle of providence on the one hand, and of free expenditure on the other; of an honourable ambition, and of elegant enjoyment. It breathes upon the face of the community, and the hollow sepulchre is forthwith beautiful to look upon.[15]

It is a piercing indictment of modern affluent societies. Everything looks proper and beautiful on the exterior: in dress, homes,

---

[12] *Idea*, 204.
[13] *Idea*, 207.
[14] *Idea*, 207.
[15] *Idea*, 207

and behavior. But much of this is vanity and dangerous self-conceit. Only after this serious criticism of a naturalist view of man did Newman write: "Hence it is that it is almost a definition of a gentleman to say he is one who never inflicts pain."[16] Of note, he specified "it is almost a definition" rather than 'it is my definition' of a gentleman.

The description is actually that of a contented, self-satisfied materialist, who avoids any inconvenience and conflict.

> The true gentleman in like manner carefully avoids whatever may cause a jar or a jolt in the minds of those with whom he is cast; - all clashing of opinion, or collision of feeling, all restraint, or suspicion, or gloom or resentment; his great concern being to make everyone at their ease and at home.[17]

Tolerance and Intolerance

Perhaps one of the most significant elements of the definition of a gentleman is his tolerance. At first glance, this seems praiseworthy because tolerance is based on respect for others and moderation in one's dealings with them. On closer examination, however, it emerges that tolerance becomes one of the principal characteristics of a gentleman, to the exclusion of the duty of correcting others' mistakes and refuting error.

It is common for people who make tolerance their highest virtue to end up being intolerant of beliefs and opinions contrary to theirs. The cause for this may lie in the fact that tolerance, for everyone and everything, is a failure in judgment of things and discrimination among things. When there is such a lack in the use of reason, it becomes easy to make one's way of thinking the standard for all others. In other words, indiscriminate tolerance can lead to intolerance of others.

In its right place, tolerance is a Christian virtue and, as such, a part of the character of a true gentleman. This virtue, however,

[16] *Idea*, 208.
[17] *Idea*, 209.

does not elude duties of justice such as discriminating true from false, good from evil. As for religious toleration, the Christian promotes the truth, rather than "look on all forms of faith with an impartial eye."[18]

In the closing paragraphs, Newman summed up his contention: "The world is content with setting right the surface of things: the Church aims at regenerating the very depths of the heart."[19] Hence, the university educates men to reason and to be gentlemen; the Church teaches them to live as Christian men:

> She is engaged with what is essential, as previous and as introductory to the ornamental and attractive. She is curing men and keeping them clear of mortal sin; she is treating of justice and chastity, and the judgment to come.[20]

The point of Newman's next Discourse, number 9, is to state that the Church has duties toward the university. The latter can form a philosopher, but it cannot form the religious mind and moral character of men. A Catholic university has the important and difficult task of educating men in these spheres, while respecting the objects and methods of the different fields of knowledge.

The True Christian Gentleman

Whereas the discourse offered the world's definition of a gentleman, it did not provide that of a Christian gentleman. Newman's definition of a Christian gentleman is to be found in his homily at the funeral of his friend James Robert Hope-Scott, a lawyer and convert to the Catholic Church. Newman wrote of him:

> He was, emphatically, a friend in need. And this same considerateness and sympathy with which he met those who asked the benefit of his opinion in matters of importance was, I believe, his characteristic in many other ways in his intercourse with those towards whom he stood in various rela-

---

[18] *Idea*, 210.
[19] *Idea*, 203.
[20] *Idea*, 203.

tions. He was always prompt, clear, decided, and disinterested. He entered into their pursuits, though dissimilar to his own; he took an interest in their objects; he adapted himself to their dispositions and tastes; he brought a strong and calm good sense to bear upon their present or their future; he aided and furthered them in their doings by his cooperation.[21]

Hope-Scott had the gift of oratory, clearness of mind, and sound judgment; he had good humor and a youthful spirit; and he used all these talents and family advantages to serve generously those in need. This magnanimity was rooted in his faith. His "heart always alive and awake at the thought of God."[22] His gifts of nature had been elevated by grace and placed at the service of men and society.

Despite the distinctions between nature and grace made in Discourse 8, this definition of a gentleman will continue to be celebrated. It is a very well-crafted literary portrayal of the prideful and material comforts praised and sought after by men in the world. A misreading of the address will ascribe this definition to Newman's ideal. Still to the very end of the discourse, he argued to the contrary:

> Such are some of the lineaments of the ethical character, which the cultivated intellect will form, apart from religious principle. They are seen within the pale of the Church and without it, in holy men, and in profligate; they form the *beau-ideal* of the world; they partly assist and partly distort the development of the Catholic. They may subserve the education of a St. Francis de Sales or a Cardinal Pole; they may be the limits of the contemplation of a Shaftesbury or a Gibbon. Basil and Julian were fellow-students at the schools of Athens; and one became the Saint and Doctor of the Church, the other her scoffing and relentless foe.[23]

[21] *OS*, 266.
[22] *OS*, 275.
[23] *Idea*, 211.

Thus, the world's idea of a gentleman is that of a man with talents, received from nature and family, and with knowledge gained by study and the exercise of natural virtues. All too often, however, this notion is rooted in pride and fosters vanity. It is lacking in the supernatural effects of grace, and many times opposed to it. The Christian gentleman, instead, is the man who models his life on Christ, his humility and charity, which guide and inspire his natural gifts and virtues.

––––––––

The following is Newman's Definition of a Gentleman in Discourse 8 of *Idea of a University.*

Hence it is that it is almost a definition of a gentleman to say he is one who never inflicts pain. This description is both refined and, as far as it goes, accurate. He is mainly occupied in merely removing the obstacles which hinder the free and unembarrassed action of those about him; and he concurs with their movements rather than takes the initiative himself. His benefits may be considered as parallel to what are called comforts or conveniences in arrangements of a personal nature: like an easy chair or a good fire, which do their part in dispelling cold and fatigue, though nature provides both means of rest and animal heat without them. The true gentleman in like manner carefully avoids whatever may cause a jar or a jolt in the minds of those with whom he is cast;—all clashing of opinion, or collision of feeling, all restraint, or suspicion, or gloom, or resentment; his great concern being to make everyone at their ease and at home. He has his eyes on all his company; he is tender towards the bashful, gentle towards the distant, and merciful towards the absurd; he can recollect to whom he is speaking; he guards against unseasonable allusions, or topics which may irritate; he is seldom prominent in conversation, and never wearisome. He makes light of favours while he does them, and seems to be receiving when he is conferring. He never speaks of himself except when compelled, never defends himself by a mere retort, he has no ears for slander or gossip, is scrupulous in imputing motives to those who interfere with him, and interprets every thing for the best. He is never mean or little in his disputes, never takes unfair advantage, never mistakes personalities or sharp sayings for arguments, or insinuates evil which he dare not say out. From a long-sighted prudence, he observes the maxim of the ancient sage, that we should ever conduct ourselves towards our enemy as if he were one day to be our friend. He has too much good sense to be affronted at insults, he is too well employed to remember injuries, and too indolent to bear malice. He is patient, forbearing, and resigned, on philosophical principles; he submits to pain, because it is inevitable, to bereavement, because it is irreparable, and to death, because it is his destiny. If he engages in controversy of any kind, his disciplined intellect preserves him from the blundering discourtesy of better, perhaps, but less educated minds; who, like blunt weapons, tear and hack instead of cutting clean, who mistake the point in argument, waste their strength on trifles, misconceive their adversary, and leave the question more involved than they find it. He may be right or wrong in his opinion, but he is too clear-headed to be unjust; he is as simple as he is forcible, and as brief as he is decisive. Nowhere shall we find greater candour, consideration, indulgence: he throws himself into the minds of his opponents, he accounts for their mistakes. He knows the weakness of human reason as well as its strength, its province and its limits. If he be an unbeliever, he will be too profound and large-minded to ridicule religion or to act against it; he is too wise to be a dogmatist or fanatic in his infidelity. He respects piety and devotion; he even supports institutions as venerable, beautiful, or useful, to which he does not assent; he honours the ministers of religion, and it contents him to decline its mysteries without assailing or denouncing them. He is a friend of religious toleration, and that, not only because his philosophy has taught him to look on all forms of faith with an impartial eye, but also from the gentleness and effeminacy of feeling, which is the attendant on civilization.

Not that he may not hold a religion too, in his own way, even when he is not a Christian. In that case his religion is one of imagination and sentiment; it is the embodiment of those ideas of the sublime, majestic, and beautiful, without which there can be no large philosophy. Sometimes he acknowledges the being of God, sometimes he invests an unknown principle or quality with the attributes of perfection. And this deduction of his reason, or creation of his fancy, he makes the occasion of such excellent thoughts, and the starting-point of so varied and systematic a teaching, that he even seems like a disciple of Christianity itself. From the very accuracy and steadiness of his logical powers, he is able to see what sentiments are consistent in those who hold any religious doctrine at all, and he appears to others to feel and to hold a whole circle of theological truths, which exist in his mind no otherwise than as a number of deductions.[24]

[24] *Idea*, 208-211.

Eleven

THE EDUCATED LAYMAN AND UNIVERSITY EDUCATION

If the Christian laity are to play their role in the world and in the Church, they need an adequate education of their minds and character. John Henry Newman dedicated his entire lifetime to education, a good number of those years engaged in university life at Oxford and Dublin, and in a school for boys at Birmingham.

In 1851 Newman gave a series of public lectures at the Corn Exchange in London, later published as *Lectures on the Present Position of Catholics in England*. In these he wished to rebut the deep prejudice against Catholics in England, which accused Catholics of superstition and fables such as that of Maria Monk[1], and all sorts of other crimes. Newman employed a masterful display of vivid imagery and strong irony to respond to impressions created in the minds of people "that a monk commits murder or adultery as readily as he eats his dinner."[2]

In the last lecture, Newman appealed to the Catholic laity to cultivate their minds, to know the faith so as to be capable of explaining it, and to prove, with their lives, that they were not what they were being falsely accused of being:

> Your strength lies in your God and your conscience; therefore it lies not in your number. (. . .) I want a laity, not arrogant, not rash in speech, not disputatious, but men who know their

---

[1] This Canadian woman published *Awful Disclosures of Maria Monk, or The Hidden Secrets of a Nun's Life in a Convent Exposed* (1836), claiming the systematic abuse of nuns by priests in Montreal and subsequent abortions of children conceived.
[2] *Pres. Pos.*, 95.

religion, who enter into it, who know just where they stand, who know what they hold and what they do not, who know their creed so well that they can give an account of it, who know so much of history that they can defend it. I want an intelligent, well-instructed laity; I am not denying you are such already; but I mean to be severe, and, as some would say, exorbitant in my demands, I wish you to enlarge your knowledge, to cultivate your reason, to get an insight into the relation of truth to truth, to learn to view things as they are, to understand how faith and reason stand to each other, what are the bases and principles of Catholicism, and where lie the main inconsistencies and absurdities of the Protestant theory.[3]

Much has been written about Newman's ideas concerning university education which retain their vibrancy and applicability today. However, as education historian Paul Shrimpton has argued, very little has been written about what Newman did in practice, to the point that people often think of his views on education as ideals that cannot be realized.[4] Shrimpton has shown how Newman was able to put theory into practice. This is the subject of the following chapter.

First we must begin by looking at the origin and content of Newman's ideas about education. Once he obtained his undergraduate degree at Trinity College at Oxford, he became a tutor and later a fellow at Oriel College. As he exercised those positions, he came to understand the teaching role of a mentor. Whereas the head of Oriel considered the mentor's role solely that of an academic advisor, Newman held that he was much more: the mentor plays a role in the moral and religious formation of students under his charge.

In this capacity as tutor, he accompanied students in the difficult transition from youth to adulthood. His students not only obtained honors; they developed their moral character and a good

---

[3] *Pres. Pos.*, 388-390.
[4] Paul Shrimpton, *The 'Making of Men': The Idea and Reality of Newman's University in Oxford and Dublin* (Leominster: Gracewing, 2014), xxxii-xxxiv.

practice of religion. A friendship developed between mentor and student that enriched both and continued after graduation.

It was in the academic and intellectual setting of Trinity College where he had done his undergraduate studies, and Oriel College where he taught, that Newman came to see the harmony between faith and reason. These apparently two separate worlds, when properly understood, were not at odds. For the same reason, a university tutor should be interested in the whole student, guiding him in his academic and moral life and not just in his studies. In this way a student integrates faith and reason in his studies and daily activities.

The dialogue between faith and reason begun by St. Anselm of Canterbury in the twelfth century has to be continued to counter what Benedict XVI called the reduction of knowledge to modern scientific knowledge. Newman made a significant contribution to this dialogue in his book *An Essay on the Idea of a University* (1858).

Oxford was the university where, in the fourteenth century, the unity of the sciences began to break with the development of the scientific method and growth of the sciences. In the sixteenth century, Newton established a paradigm for knowledge that challenged and seemed to surpass the knowledge attained through philosophy and theology.

Based on this notion of precise measurements and formulas, Descartes discarded any 'certainty' based on testimony and authority. As a result, in the late eighteenth century, Paley wished to prove the existence of God from the argument of design, as if God's existence relied on scientific proofs. In the same century, John Locke attacked the importance of a classical education in favor of the sciences and new schools of thought.

Newman challenged the assumptions that give the new sciences superiority. He explained that each science has its object, its method, and its instruments. To confuse one with another leads to the absurdity that would allow one to think that a chemist is, by virtue of his profession, necessarily a good cook. In the discourses that Newman gave at the Catholic University of Ireland, he helped the students and faculty to recognize the limits of each science, and the role of philosophy and theology in university education. For us to grasp Newman's way of thinking, we should mention, albeit briefly, the influence that Bishop Joseph Butler's *Analogy of Religion, Natural and Revealed, to the Constitution and Course of Nature* (1736) made on him when he read it after his Anglican ordination in 1825.[5] Butler confirmed Newman's understanding of the fundamental structure of the world, its reality and mystery. According to the *Analogy*, we should expect and recognize the presence of mystery everywhere. Commenting on its influence on Newman, Louis Bouyer explains this central teaching of Butler that calls for harmony between faith and reason:

> The visible world itself, properly considered, is a mystery so great and of such a nature that it should teach us not to be troubled by mysteries, and in particular by the mystery we encounter in the very core of Revelation. This very mystery is perhaps the surest evidence that it does indeed proceed from the Author of Nature himself.[6]

Just as Butler wrote about the reconciliation of faith and reason, so too did St. John Paul II in the twentieth century. In the encyclical letter *Fides et ratio*, St. John Paul II offered a long reflection on the unity of faith and reason, and the need to recover this vision of knowledge. In doing so he mentioned Newman first in a list of important modern thinkers who have contributed to this effort.[7] The pope suggested that the relationship between theolo-

---

[5] Joseph Butler (1692-1752), a theologian and moral philosopher, was first Bishop of Bristol and later of Durham. He argued against deism by asserting that by analogy with patterns observable both in nature and human affairs which we hold as probable we can also hold as probable the revealed truths of Christianity.

[6] Louis Bouyer, 79. For a good explanation of Butler's influence on Newman, see pp. 77-80. He indicates, for instance, how Butler takes this idea from the early Christian writer Origen.

[7] "We see the same fruitful relationship between philosophy and the word of God in the courageous research pursued by more recent thinkers, among whom I gladly mention, in a Western context, figures such as John Henry Newman, Antonio Rosmini, Jacques Maritain, Étienne Gilson and Edith Stein and, in an Eastern context, eminent scholars such as Vladimir S. Soloviev, Pavel A. Florensky, Petr Chaadaev and Vladimir N. Lossky." John Paul II, Encyclical Letter *Fides et ratio*, (September 14, 1998), n. 74. Vatican website : www.vatican.va.

gy and philosophy (faith and reason) could be best construed as a circle:

> It is as if, moving between the twin poles of God's word and a better understanding of it, reason is offered guidance and is warned against paths which would lead it to stray from revealed Truth and to stray in the end from the truth pure and simple. Instead, reason is stirred to explore paths which of itself it would not even have suspected it could take. This circular relationship with the word of God leaves philosophy enriched, because reason discovers new and unsuspected horizons.[8]

The origin of Newman's lectures is tied to the British Government's conciliatory plan towards Ireland in 1854 to establish the Queen's University of Ireland. Until then, Irish Catholics who pursued university studies only had one university in Dublin, the Anglican Trinity College, where religious tests were still in force. The new university would be secular and nondenominational. Only a few Irish bishops agreed with the idea of "mixed education" of Protestants and Catholics. As a result, Rome forbade the Irish hierarchy from being part of such a university and urged the establishment of a Catholic university similar to that of Louvain in Belgium, reestablished in 1835.

A committee for the Catholic university was established and Paul Cullen—then Archbishop of Armagh and, soon after, Archbishop of Dublin—became its head. In July 1850, he visited Newman at Birmingham on two occasions to speak with him about the project. On the second visit he invited Newman to become the university's first rector. After painstaking delays for Newman, the nascent institution would open its doors in the fall of 1854.

Two years earlier, at Cullen's invitation, Newman gave a series of lectures to promote the project of the university in Dublin. He delivered five lectures on successive weeks. Over time, these lec-

---

[8] John Paul II, *Fides et ratio*, 73.

tures, and others, which Newman gave for the opening of various schools within the university, were published in one volume titled *An Essay on the Idea of a University.*

Idea of the University and the Liberal Arts

The eight discourses, which make up the first part of the essay, justify the reason for a liberal arts education, a tradition of education dating back to the ancient Greeks and Romans, which 'privileged' the liberal arts over the servile arts.

In Discourse 2, Newman made the claim that will be repeated throughout his lectures:

> Religious doctrine is knowledge, in as full a sense as Newton's doctrine is knowledge. University Teaching without Theology is simply unphilosophical. Theology has at least as good a right to claim a place there as Astronomy.[9]

In Discourse 3 he explained how knowledge consists in one circle of truths which "taken together form one integral subject for contemplation, so there are no natural or real limits between part and part; one is ever running into another."[10]

Thus Newman considered that sciences are partial views or abstractions, by which the mind looks upon its object. Sciences are partial and incomplete, and by reason of their incompleteness, sciences are interconnected: each science needs the others.

He explained that we can study man in a variety of relations, which constitute sciences—for example, politics, economics, medicine, theology, etc. When we study man according to all these and other relations, we study him as a whole; but if we do not take him as a whole, the defect is greater or lesser in proportion than the relation which is omitted. This is also the case with sciences, such as in pure mathematics, "the conclusions of Anatomy, Chemistry, Dynamics, and other sciences, are revised and

[9] *Idea*, 42.
[10] *Idea*, 45.

completed by each other.[11] "Newtonian physics, for instance, depends on metaphysical concepts such as: "that there is such a thing as matter, that our senses are trustworthy, that there is a logic of induction, and so on."[12]

Newman held that the exclusion of theology from the circle of knowledge is not only indefensible but harmful to the rest of the sciences. When scientists exclude sciences other than their own,

> they necessarily become bigots and quacks, scorning all principles and reported facts which do not belong to their own pursuit, and thinking to effect everything without aid from any other quarter.[13]

There is, according to Newman and earlier thinkers, one science that measures and integrates the other sciences. He calls it "a science of sciences":

> the comprehension of the bearings of one science on another, and the use of each to each, and the location and limitation and adjustment and due appreciation of them all, one with another, this belongs, I conceive, to a sort of science distinct from all of them, and in some sense a science of sciences, which is my own conception of what is meant by Philosophy, in the true sense of the word.[14]

After presenting the analogy of university knowledge with a circle, he discussed the place of theology in the circle of knowledge. He argued that assuming the existence of God and man,

> (. . .) no University Professor, who had suppressed in physical lectures the idea of volition, who did not take volition for granted, could escape a one-sided, a radically false view of the things which he discussed; not indeed that his own definitions, principles, and laws would be wrong, or his abstract statements, but his considering his own study to be the key of

---

[11] *Idea*, 48-49.
[12] *Idea*, 49.
[13] *Idea*, 50.
[14] *Idea*, 51.

everything that takes place on the face of the earth, and his passing over anthropology, this would be his error." Such a professor would "no longer (be) a teacher of liberal knowledge, but a narrow-minded bigot.[15]

Newman asserted that,

> If the creature is ever setting in motion an endless series of physical causes and effects, much more is the Creator; and as our excluding volition from our range of ideas is a denial of the soul, so our ignoring Divine Agency is a virtual denial of God.[16]

Newman pointed out how the omission of theology will lead to its place being usurped by other sciences, with a consequent damage to the whole system of knowledge.

In this Discourse 3, he defined the term "theology," first by stating what it is not: it is not so-called physical theology (religious remarks upon the physical world), nor is it the "Evidences of Religion" advanced by Paley. Neither is theology a vague notion of Christianity nor a simple acquaintance with Scripture. By "theology," Newman meant "the Science of God, or the truths we know about God put into a system; just as we have a science of the stars, and call it astronomy, or of the crust of the earth, and call it geology."[17]

The same argument is taken up in Discourse 4, where Newman asserted that when a science tries to become the sole exponent of all things, it falls into error by ". . . encroaching on territory not its own, and undertaking problems which it has no instruments to solve."[18]

Newman described the work of the human mind: to grasp the form of things, to discern what is beautiful and what is not; to give meaning to things, to distinguish between rule and exception, to assign phenomena to a general law and effects to a cause—

[15] *Idea*, 58.
[16] *Idea*, 59.
[17] *Idea*, 61.
[18] *Idea*, 74.

in a word, to philosophize. But man is impatient with ignorance and, without sufficient data, pronounces judgments and offers absurd interpretations of events.

Men who cultivate one science or method of thought have no more right, though they often have more ambition:

> (. . .) to generalize upon the basis of their own pursuit but beyond its range, than the schoolboy or the ploughman to judge of a Prime Minister. But they must have something to say on every subject; habit, fashion, the public require it of them: and, if so, they can only give sentence according to their knowledge.[19]

He referred to Aristotle, Cicero, and Bacon, who criticize the man who acts with the obstinacy of bigots and becomes "a person of one idea," "a man of one science." The principles of this science, true to a certain point, degenerate into error and quackery because they are carried to excess "inasmuch as a little science is not deep philosophy."[20]

But Newman went further; he wished to make the point that the exclusion of theology from universal knowledge is not only a loss to theology,

> (. . .) it is the perversion of other sciences. What it unjustly forfeits, others unjustly seize. They have their own department, and, in going out of it, attempt to do what they really cannot do."[21]

Newman illustrated the error of sciences overstepping their limits by referring to the remarks of a distinguished professor of comparative anatomy who denied the immateriality of the soul. Newman did not doubt the physician's respect for another's religious opinion nor his desire to avoid censure. Newman commented:

---

[19] *Idea*, 76.
[20] *Idea*, 77.
[21] *Idea*, 78.

What then must have been his fault or mistake, but that he unsuspiciously threw himself upon his own particular science, which is of a material character, and allowed it to carry him forward into a subject-matter, where it had no right to give the law, viz., that of spiritual beings, which directly belongs to the science of Theology?[22]

He offered illustrations of similar errors from history, geology and other sciences. With regard to the science of political economy, he noted that it is not a sin to make money but that since love of money is the root of all evils, this science could also be an occasion of sin; it needs the "control of Revealed Truth." He wrote,

> In theory the science of economy can determine the method of gaining wealth, but it cannot determine "that it is the way to be virtuous and the price of happiness" which would be surpassing its bounds.[23]

Discourse 5, titled "Knowledge an End in Itself," one of the hardest to grasp, offers one of the principal concepts of the *Idea of a University* in the following words: "Liberal Education, viewed in itself, is simply the cultivation of the intellect, as such, and its object is nothing more or less than intellectual excellence."[24]

Here also, Newman followed his teacher, Aristotle, specifically in his notion that everything has its own perfection, and he illustrated this with an example from gardening:

> Why do you take such pains with your garden or your park? You see to your walks and turf and shrubberies; to your trees and drives; not as if you meant to make an orchard of the one, or corn or pasture land of the other, but because there is a special beauty in all that is goodly in wood, water, plain, and slope, brought all together by art into one shape, and grouped into one whole.[25]

[22] *Idea*, 85.
[23] *Idea*, 87-88.
[24] *Idea*, 121.
[25] *Idea*, 121-122.

Newman continued:

> "There is a physical beauty and a moral: there is a beauty of person, there is a beauty of our moral being, which is natural virtue; and in like manner there is a beauty, there is a perfection, of the intellect."[26]

Just as there is beauty in art, heroes, and saints, there is beauty also in the intellect, of which he wrote:

> To open the mind, to correct it, to refine it, to enable it to know, and to digest, master, rule, and use its knowledge, to give it power over its own faculties, application, flexibility, method, critical exactness, sagacity, resource, address, eloquent expression, is an object as intelligible (for here we are inquiring, not what the object of a Liberal Education is worth, nor what use the Church makes of it, but what it is in itself), I say, an object as intelligible as the cultivation of virtue, while, at the same time, it is absolutely distinct from it.[27]

After describing the beauty and range of the intellect, Newman argued that this knowledge is a sufficient end in itself. It is commonly called "liberal arts" or "liberal education." And by contrast to servile work, which involves the body and machines, "liberal education and liberal pursuits are exercises of mind, of reason, of reflection."[28] This knowledge is good in itself, without ulterior ends. He did not deny the good or the merit of useful knowledge, but he wished to point out that there is *knowledge*, which is its own reward.

In other discourses, Newman pointed out how a liberal arts education has important consequences for society, but he labored to defend its own good as a perfection of the mind.

The value of such a liberal arts education in favor of the useful knowledge of mechanical sciences had been strongly challenged at Oxford at the turn of the nineteenth century and would once

[26] *Idea*, 122.
[27] *Idea*, 122-123.
[28] *Idea*, 107.

more be placed in doubt in the last quarter of the century. This is the subject of Discourse 7, titled "Knowledge Viewed in Relation to Professional Skill," in which Newman ascribed blame to the Edinburgh Review for its attack on classical education, and to John Locke, whom he quoted as follows:

> Reason, if consulted with, would advise, that their children's time should be spent in acquiring what might be useful to them, when they come to be men, rather than that their heads should be stuffed with a deal of trash, a great part whereof they usually never do ('tis certain they never need to) think on again as long as they live.[29]

Newman wrote that the mission of the philosopher of utility "was the increase of physical enjoyment and social comfort and most wonderfully, most awfully has he fulfilled his conception and his design."[30] He acknowledged that this philosophy provides for all of us food, health and general well-being. But Newman lamented that, in his time, the philosophers of utility "depreciate, or trample on Theology."[31]

Next, true to his line of reasoning, Newman indicated the limits of philosophy. Reason is not the same as virtue. Knowledge contributes to make men better, but it does not replace religion:

> Knowledge is one thing, virtue is another; good sense is not conscience, refinement is not humility, nor is largeness and justness of view faith. Philosophy, however enlightened, however profound, gives no command over the passions, no influential motives, no vivifying principles. Liberal Education makes not the Christian, not the Catholic, but the gentleman.[32]

He explained that qualities of "large knowledge," what the world considers a gentleman and the goal of a university education, al-

[29] *Idea*, 159.
[30] *Idea*, 118.
[31] *Idea*, 118
[32] *Idea*, 120.

though good, are not a guarantee of holiness or even conscientiousness. Newman then presented readers with a beautiful analogy to illustrate this:

> Quarry the granite rock with razors, or moor the vessel with a thread of silk; then may you hope with such keen and delicate instruments as human knowledge and human reason to contend against those giants, the passion and the pride of man.[33]

This very idea would be developed in Discourse 8 where, as was seen in the previous chapter, Newman showed how far the university can go in forming "a gentleman." Religion, specifically revealed religion, with its truths, precepts and sacraments, is needed to make of the gentleman a saint or someone who pursues the ideal of holiness.

Before that, in Discourse 6, Newman had discussed knowledge in relation to learning. This is a subject germane to today's university environment, where we find a plethora of facts and courses but almost always disconnected and without any hierarchy of knowledge.

To begin with, Newman considered that the perfection of the intellect is not properly called wisdom, knowledge or science. He gave it the name of philosophy, philosophical knowledge, enlargement of mind, or illumination. Newman thought that the end of a university is the education of the intellect—or to foster an intellectual culture. A university can be an instrument of the Church, such as the Catholic University of Ireland, which Newman helped to establish, but in the first place it has the object and mission of educating the intellect. "It educates the intellect to reason well in all matters, to reach out towards truth, and to grasp it."[34]

Contrary to this view, in the second half of the nineteenth century, more people began to consider that a university was a place for acquiring as much knowledge as possible on a great many subjects. This notion starts with the education given boys in school and carries on to the university where people hold . . .

[33] *Idea*, 121.
[34] *Idea*, 125–126.

(. . .) that there is no true culture without acquirements, and that philosophy presupposes knowledge. It requires a great deal of reading, or a wide range of information, to warrant us in putting forth our opinions on any serious subject; and without such learning the most original mind may be able indeed to dazzle, to amuse, to refute, to perplex, but not to come to any useful result or any trustworthy conclusion.[35]

Naturally Newman admitted the need for learning, but tried to show by examples that the enlargement of the mind is more than the acquisition of knowledge. He pointed out that a great intellect like that of Aristotle, Thomas Aquinas or Newton . . .

(. . .) takes a connected view of old and new, past and present, far and near, and which has an insight into the influence of all these one on another; without which there is no whole, and no centre. (. . .) possesses the knowledge, not only of things, but also of their mutual and true relations; knowledge, not merely considered as acquirement, but as philosophy.[36]

He explained that great memory, for instance, does not make a philosopher. Someone can possess a lot of information such as a scientist, a historian or a lawyer, but this does not guarantee the absence of narrowness of mind.

Men who have seen much of the world and of people may have a lot of information, but they do not necessarily have a great intellect or culture. This is what often happens to students in our modern universities. They are lost, as someone in the woods or in a maze, or as someone in a city without a map.[37]

For a majority of students today, the result of higher education is a smattering of disconnected subjects. So many of these students leave the university with a shallow grasp of a multiplicity of

---

[35] *Idea*, 129.

[36] *Idea*, 134.

[37] In some universities students study a chapter or more of this classical text by Newman. A recent anthology of texts has been prepared by Paula Jullian who has paraphrased each lecture. See *La Idea de una Universidad de J.H. Newman. Traducción Editada de Pasajes Escogidos*, (Santiago: Ediciones UC., 2015).

subjects "and so shallow as not even to know their shallowness."[38]

Overall the series of lectures by Newman were very well received. In the course of the century that has transpired since their delivery, they have become a classic of university education and English prose. Their impressive content, however, is well known to experts only and considered by many others as something of the past. On the contrary, they constitute a clear and imposing vision of the complete whole of university education or "circle of knowledge," to use Newman's words.

The university's mission is to form and enlarge the minds of students, educating them with a philosophical habit of mind, instructing them on the limits and cooperation between the sciences, and the role of philosophy "as a sort of science of sciences."[39]

Now we must turn to Newman's implementation of these educational ideas, his successes and failures at the university in Dublin and, later, at a school for boys in Birmingham.

---

[38] *Idea*, 149.

[39] Some of Newman's notions are consonant with those espoused a century later by Josemaría Escrivá, who also founded a university—the University of Navarre—and directly inspired the establishment of other ones. For a comparison of their educational principles and practices see Juan R. Vélez G, "Newman and Escrivá: Two Distinguished Educators," *Faith and Reason*, Vol. XXVII, (2002),195-215.

Twelve

THE MAKING OF MEN
AND THE REALITY OF A
UNIVERSITY EDUCATION

Today when most universities are completely disconnected departments—often driven by research and with very little or no concern for forming the intellect and the character of students—we must ask if the university envisioned by Newman is actually possible. More to the point, was Newman able to create a liberal arts university that accomplished the ideals that he voiced in his lectures on the scope and nature of a university?

Newman was founder and rector of the Catholic University of Ireland for four years (1854-1858). During this time he opened various schools within the university and established four residence halls or collegiate houses. In this period, the enrollment grew even though it remained small overall.[1] He recruited teachers from talented English converts to Catholicism, as well as some distinguished professors. In the same period, he designed and built a university church. Newman directed all of this rapid growth at the same time that he prepared statutes for the government of the university, curricula, study programs and examinations.

The university opened on Friday, November 3, 1854, with entrance exams. On November 5, Newman addressed the seventeen

---

[1] On opening day, seventeen students were enrolled. At the end of the first term, the list rose to twenty-seven. The Lent term began with thirty-seven, and by the end of first year, around sixty students in total had matriculated, even though some came and went. See *The Making of Men*, 179.

students who passed, and classes began the following day. Robert Ormsby, professor of classical literature, took notes of Newman's memorable words. Newman told the students that although they had come to the university to prepare for the professions they chose, there was a more important reason why they had come. They had come to become men. They could learn the professions at other places, but this they would learn at the university better than at any other place.

The rector illustrated his point with a story about a mother with children who was widowed and left without means. When one of her sons was offered a job below his expectations and had thoughts of declining it, his mother advised him to reconsider, because 'it is not the place that makes the man, but the man that makes the place.' Newman explained that a man would be valued wherever he was if he was 'well educated, of cultivated mind, well principled and gentleman-like.' He asserted that, provided a man had an honest trade and profession and discharged his duties well, it would not matter where he worked. 'A gentleman carries his own recommendation with him' he said.

Newman was committed to forming each student as a whole, his intellect and character. He told the first students:

> Professions differ, and what is an education for one youth is not the education for another; but there is one education which all should have in common, and which is distinct from the education which is given to fit each for his profession. It is the education which made the man; it does not make physicians, surgeons, or engineers, or soldiers, or bankers, or merchants, but it makes men. It is that education which enables the man to adorn the place, instead of the place adorning the man. And this is the education for which you especially come to the University—it is to be made men.[2]

---

[2] John Henry Newman, *My Campaign in Ireland*, ed. William P. Neville, [1923], 314-315, quoted in *The Making of Men*, 175-176.

A liberal arts education, as described by Newman in the *Idea of a University*, was fundamental to educating the intellect—forming a philosophical habit of mind with the capacity to analyze, differentiate, compare, reach conclusions, articulate ideas and adopt principles. Yet all this was not sufficient to "make the man," to forge character, correcting and guiding the passions, and instilling religious truths and practices. For this, Newman felt, students needed the guidance of tutors, and an environment that was morally safe and intellectually stimulating. The best place, in his experience, was a college or collegiate house within a university.

A series of articles he wrote for the Catholic University *Gazette*, a school newspaper he founded and directed, complement the ideas he put forth in the *Idea of a University Education*. In these articles, later titled *The Rise and Progress of Universities*, he wrote of two rival powers that he called "influence" and "discipline" or "system." Newman believed a university began with the personal influence exerted by teachers but it required a system to preserve its gains. By the latter he was referring to a collegiate system. He explained:

> It was taken to mean a place of residence for the University student, who would there find himself under the guidance and instruction of Superiors and Tutors, bound to attend to his personal interests, moral and intellectual.[3]

He further explained that the Edinburgh Review, which he called "the party of the North and of progress,"

> (. . .) have ever advocated the Professorial system, as it has been called, and have pointed in their own behalf to the practice of the middle ages and of modern Germany and France; the party of the South and of prescription have ever stood up for the Tutorial or collegiate system, and have pointed to

[3] John Henry Newman, "Professors and Tutors" in "The Rise and Progress of Universities," *HS*, Vol. 3:182.

Protestant Oxford and Cambridge, where it has almost or altogether superseded the Professorial. Now I have on former
occasions said enough to show that I am for both views at
once, and think neither of them complete without the other.
I admire the Professor, I venerate the College. The Professorial system fulfils the strict idea of a University, and is sufficient for its *being*, but it is not sufficient for its *well-being*.
Colleges constitute the *integrity* of a University.

The model adopted by Newman for the Catholic University of
Ireland was a combination of the tutorial system at Oxford and
Cambridge and the magisterial system in parts of Europe. He had
firsthand experience of the first and knew about the second. He
did not include the research system of the German universities
that later inspired many of the American universities, starting
with John Hopkins. He thought that research was primarily the
work of research institutes or societies.

A few years earlier, royal commissioners investigating Oxford
had also concluded in their *Report and Evidence* (1853) that it was
beneficial to combine the two rival systems—the professorial and
the tutorial.[4] An outspoken opponent of the report was Pusey,
who thought that this would tend toward the destruction of the
collegiate system.

Although the rector wished to have a residential university with
colleges, as was the case in Oxford and Cambridge, he settled for
a mixed residential and nonresidential system, realizing that this
was necessary to increase enrollment since many students had
family residing in Dublin. But in his mind, the reason for university residences or collegiate houses was paramount to the point
that the nonresidential students were assigned to a residence even
though they lived off campus. For Newman, the residence was an
important place of learning for students—providing a setting
where students could learn from one another in the course of
many different interactions, including conversations at meals and
through sports. Within this arrangement, students had the super-

---

[4] *The Making of Men*, 126.

vision of an upperclassman and of a tutor. Each house was presided over by a dean who was a priest. Newman himself was dean of St. Mary's, one of the houses.

From the start, Newman thought of forming an English house with the sons of his friends, drawing young men from the higher classes and nobility.[5] With his reputation he managed to attract to the house youths from various countries like England, Scotland, France, and Ireland. At the age of fifty-three, the university rector also occupied himself finding and furnishing a house, and then supervising the servants and attending to the domestic finances.

Despite tight finances, Newman was able to maintain the semblance of 'high table' at St. Mary's where, besides the students, he entertained many visitors on university business. Aside from the visits of guests, and unlike the other houses, Newman provided the students with wine for dinner.[6] He also allowed his residents a great degree of liberty, such as going out at night but always accompanied. All of this occasioned gossip about Newman's practices and brought upon him opposition by the bishops.

At St. Mary's, Newman also took on the duties of chaplain and tutor. Thus rather than distancing himself from the students, he was directly involved in their pastoral care. Education, for him, was something personal where the teacher guided the reading of a student, discussed difficulties, encouraged, and corrected. As an educator, he was patient and lenient with students, avoiding harsh measures. Instead, he tried to win his students over when they did not fulfill their duties. The students, however, tried his patience, especially with their spending habits and idleness during vacations. He was obliged to write Lord Henry Kerr about the inordinate spending of his son Ralph, and even had to remove from St. Mary's the son of Lord Charles Thynne for his poor behavior. As a priest, he helped his students live the faith and exercise piety. Mass was said every day with some students in attendance, and the Blessed Sacrament was reserved in the tabernacle of the chapel.[7]

---

[5] *The Making of Men*, 184-197.
[6] *The Making of Men*, 188.
[7] JHN to Lord Henry Ker,(January 30, 1855), *LD*, Vol. 16: 370.

In the articles for the *Gazette*, Newman explained why a collegiate house was so important for students who often moved to a new city, away from the supervision of family, and were tempted to moral excesses. For him, the house or college was like a home, and those in charge were like foster parents. After the students would leave the university, the college would bring fond memories to their minds and hold a dear place in their hearts. Newman wrote:

> It is all, and does all, which is implied in the name of home. Youths, who have left the paternal roof, and travelled some hundred miles for the acquisition of knowledge, find an "altera Troja" and "simulata Pergama" at the end of their journey and in their place of temporary sojourn. Home is for the young, who know nothing of the world, and who would be forlorn and sad, if thrown upon it. (. . .) It is the providential shelter of the weak and inexperienced, who have still to learn how to cope with the temptations which lie outside of it.[8]

The collegiate houses that Newman envisioned and set up at the Catholic University differ significantly from dorms and fraternity houses in contemporary North American universities. The former were small households that provided an environment of study as well as religious practices and afforded close supervision by adults. The latter are large residences, often morally corrupting, having little or poor adult supervision. The collegiate houses in Newman's time were intended 'to make the students men.'

The lectures were held in classrooms in the University House, the largest of the houses, which doubled as the main university building. Like the other university buildings, it was an elegant house, purchased in 1853. The university began with morning and afternoon lectures in classics, mathematics, and modern languages. In the evenings there were lectures on Sacred Scripture, Spanish poetry, Irish literature, or classical literature. During the first year, the evening classes were open to the public, including women.

[8] *HS*, Vol. 3: 214.

Newman, who had been an examiner at Oxford, gave great importance to examinations, a fact indicated by the amount of time—eleven days the first year!—he set aside for examining the students. He acted as one of the examiners. The official university examinations were scheduled for the second and fourth years, but to ensure that students would keep up with their studies, he established regular testing at the end of each term.

As was to be expected, the nascent university included a library from the start and soon began to receive gifts and large bequests of books, such as the library of the recently deceased then Archbishop of Dublin, Daniel Murray; a collection of around five hundred books from a recently deceased priest; and 192 volumes on civil and canon law donated by James Hope-Scott.[9] These were catalogued by the secretary of the university acting as librarian.

Naturally, the university needed a center for its religious life, similar to what St. Mary the Virgin was at Oxford University. With his own funds Newman commissioned and helped design and build a church on St. Stephen's Green. He entrusted the architectural task to John Hungerford Pollen, a convert from Anglicanism, whom he had appointed to the chair of fine arts. The beautiful church, with its byzantine style and colored Irish marble, was completed and consecrated by Archbishop Cullen with the title *Sedes Sapientiae* on Ascension Thursday, May 1, 1856. From its pulpit Newman delivered memorable homilies on various occasions. At the first one, on the feast of St. Monica, the mother of St. Augustine, he compared St. Monica as a type or image of the Church who labored to bring her intelligent son back to the faith. He explained that a primary task of the Catholic University was to assist the Church in caring for her student family.

Newman spoke of a common temptation of students to turn away from religious principles and practices:

His curiosity now takes a new turn; he listens to views and discussions which are inconsistent with the sanctity of religious faith. At first he has no temptation to adopt them; only he wishes to know what is "said." As time goes on, however, living with companions who have no fixed principle, and who, if they do not oppose, at least do not take for granted, any the most elementary truths; or worse, hearing or reading what is directly against religion, at length, without being conscious of it, he admits a sceptical influence upon his mind. He does not know it, he does not recognize it, but there it is; and, *before* he recognizes it, it leads him to a fretful, impatient way of speaking of the persons, conduct, words, and measures of religious men or of men in authority.[10]

Newman added that students could easily fall prey to the false idea of an inherent separation between reason and faith:

This is a very serious state of things; and what makes it worse is, that these various faculties and powers of the human mind have so long been separated from each other, so long cultivated and developed each by itself, that it comes to be taken for granted that they cannot be united; and it is commonly thought, because some men follow duty, others pleasure, others glory, and others intellect, therefore that one of these things excludes the other; that duty cannot be pleasant, that virtue cannot be intellectual, that goodness cannot be great (. . .)[11]

At the time of revolution and intellectual skepticism prevalent in parts of continental Europe, he cautioned against the temptation of fleeing from the world to the Church. Instead, guided by the Church, students must consider that their knowledge should be in harmony with religious faith:

I wish the intellect to range with the utmost freedom, and religion to enjoy an equal freedom; but what I am stipulating for is, that they should be found in one and the same place, and exemplified in the same persons. I want to destroy that diversity of centres, which puts everything into confusion by

[10] *OS*, 10-11.
[11] *OS*, 8-9.

creating a contrariety of influences. I wish the same spots and the same individuals to be at once oracles of philosophy and shrines of devotion.[12]

Further, Newman felt that the boys who were becoming men needed a firm hand together with freedom and space to think and act.

Let both influences act freely, and then, as a general rule, no system of mere religious guardianship which neglects the Reason, will in matter of fact succeed against the School. Youths need a masculine religion, if it is to carry captive their restless imaginations, and their wild intellects, as well as to touch their susceptible hearts.[13]

Newman gave great importance to the informal learning that went on outside of lectures and tutorials. A few months before the university began, he conceived of a "debating society," which gave rise to the Historic, Literary. and Aesthetical Society.[14] Even though Trinity College in Dublin had a Historical Society, Newman's creation was novel in the nineteenth century.[15] In an unpublished article in 1819, he proposed the establishment of a debating society for Oxford undergraduates that would meet to debate on a whole range of matters including history, poetry, and fine arts, excluding only politics of the last 100 years.

In keeping with Newman's vision, the association was a private society entirely run by the students—even though it was very likely that Newman helped the students to prepare an elaborate set of statutes. The members wrote papers and compositions, delivered speeches, and responded with criticism to the literary compositions or spoke in debate. The meetings, according to New-

---

[12] *OS*, 13.
[13] *OS*, 14.
[14] See a detailed account of this society in *The Making of Men*, 258-263.
[15] At Oxford, a debating society, a forerunner of the Oxford Union (1830), was active in 1823-1825. The Cambridge Union debating society began in 1815 but was discontinued in 1817 and resumed in 1821, providing there would be no political discussion of matters from the preceding twenty years. See *The Making of Men*, 285.

man, afforded the opportunity "for the cultivation of taste, and the development of the imaginative and inventive powers of the mind."[16] They were intended to help students to exercise creative thought, offer criticism, develop the capacity of speaking extempore, and write well. The society attracted student leaders and improved their talents. An example of such a student was the second president of the society, Henry Bethell, nephew of Sir Richard Bethell, Britain's attorney-general. Henry had studied at Eton, which he left upon becoming Catholic.

Newman's insistence on the importance of the liberal arts and the formation of a philosophical habit of mind did not mean that he ignored the growth of the practical sciences and their interest in society. Under his leadership the university opened schools of medicine, sciences, and engineering. The medical school was a success almost from its incorporation to the university.[17] From the start he hoped to establish a faculty of law and also of theology.[18] He attempted to start the law school but was unsuccessful because students who went to Trinity or the Queen's Colleges were allowed to take the bar with fewer years of study.

Another contribution to higher education attempted by Newman at Dublin was to place laymen in charge of finances and other administrative responsibilities at the university. He thought laymen would be better suited than priests for these roles, but he met with opposition from Archbishop Cullen on this and on the appointment of the vice-rector of the university and the deans of the houses. Newman wanted to suggest the appointment of a vice-rector who would understand his vision of education. However, without even consulting with Newman, on successive occasions Cullen appointed those whom he wanted. These men and Newman got on well but worked along different lines that impeded a good outcome. The fact was that Cullen, despite his good intentions and determination to establish the Catholic University,

---

[16] Preface to the rulebook for the Historical, Literary, and Aesthetical Society. See *The Making of Men*, 259.
[17] Newman also established a house for medical students similar to the other houses.
[18] *The Making of Men*, 204.

did not share Newman's vision and did not fully trust him. Cullen wanted to run the university more like a seminary or something like the Irish College in Rome.

Archbishop Cullen often delayed months in replying to the rector's letters and did not back him sufficiently. Exhausted by this lack of cooperation and burdened by matters at the Birmingham Oratory of which Newman remained the head, he decided to resign as rector of the university. The university had become a reality, but it was a fledgling institution. Without Newman's prestige and leadership, it would not continue to grow and attract sufficient students. But already during Newman's tenure as rector, the university had failed to enroll the needed number of students. This was due to various reasons, including the impoverishment of the general population and the fact that wealthy Catholic families still preferred to send their sons to study at Trinity College, Dublin, or abroad. Failure to obtain a charter from the crown, in great part due to resistance by the bishops to have laymen in the governing body of the university, also impeded the growth of the university.

Given the English control of Ireland, the country was not ready for a Catholic university. In addition to the clerical mindset of the clergy—which was an impediment for the granting of the charter by the British government—famine and political agitation in Ireland made the growth of the university very difficult. The university established by Newman under Cullen was incorporated years later in 1909 into University College, Dublin, as a part of the then newly established National University of Ireland.

John Hungerford Pollen wrote of Newman's vision for the university:

> Neither was the institution with its colleges a seminary. It was a gymnasium for the formation of character, and the training of the intellect. It had to exercise its youth in the right use of *moral* restraint; to prepare them for that full liberty which awaited them when the University life was ended. They had to learn the right use of the reasoning powers, and to appreci-

ate the confidence placed in their honour. The fact that such a liberty is sometimes abused in the old Universities did not frighten Newman.[19]

As Paul Shrimpton has demonstrated well, Newman made a reality what he had put forth in his *Idea of a University* and *Historical Sketches*. He left us a compelling legacy that highlights the importance of a liberal arts education and the role of personal mentoring as well as the value of small and formative student residences. As the first rector of the Catholic University of Ireland, he helped faculty and students to see the harmony between faith and reason, and, albeit with limited success, advocated the role of laymen in Catholic higher education.

[19] *The Making of Men*, 474.

Thirteen

EDUCATING BOYS AND THE ORATORY SCHOOL

The education of children and youth is as delicate as it is challenging. John Henry Newman was especially suited for this work, and he did not spare any effort or love for this task. It is no surprise that he was involved in the education of boys, but his involvement came after he had been a university teacher and rector of a university. It was during the last years of his life that he dedicated his energy and applied his long experience to this enterprise.

In the early nineteenth century only a small number of schools for boys who had completed grammar school existed in England. The more established ones, which assured students of social connections, were Protestant institutions such as Eton, Harrow, and Westminster. These so-called public schools were characterized by being large boarding schools in rural settings, set up primarily for the upper classes and giving much importance to the liberty and self-governance of students under a prefect system.[1] Among the English public schools, the most well known was Eton. Student bullying and rebellion against the teachers, as well cruel punishments such as flogging, were common in these schools, something that prompted a reform in the 1820s and 1830s.[2]

The other schools were Catholic ones that, for the most part, were seminaries, which also allowed enrollment for students not

---

[1] See Paul Shrimpton's *A Catholic Eton? Newman's Oratory School*, (Leominster, England: Gracewing, 2005), 10-34. This book is a very good and detailed account of the establishment of the Oratory School and its course during Newman's life.

[2] Thomas Arnold, (1795-1842), the head of Rugby, was one of the leaders of this reform, which—based on religious principles—led to discipline and academic excellence. See *A Catholic Eton?*, 13.

aspiring to the priesthood. The first group excelled in academics but were very lax in discipline and morals. The latter schools were not as good academically and functioned like seminaries with excessive student supervision.

After the establishment of the Birmingham Oratory, Newman dreamed of starting a school for boys on a property called St. Wilfrid's, which was inherited by the Oratorians. It could be called an "Eton of the Oratory" providing future vocations for the Oratory. But the plan petered out when the London Oratory failed to back the venture.

In 1857, after notifying the Irish bishops of his intention to resign from the Catholic University in Dublin, Newman once again began to consider plans for a school for boys. His friends did not wish to send their children to public schools, yet wished for them to receive a comparable education to prepare for university studies and professional schools. John Hungerford Pollen, who had taught at the Catholic University in Dublin, was one of these friends who sought Newman's advice on how to educate his sons. Newman advised him to have those interested form a trust with a fund and to keep a low profile, avoiding the jealousy of existing Catholic schools. He suggested starting with a school for young boys and after five or so years deciding on the question of whether or not to continue with a public school for older boys.

Newman discussed the idea with Sir John Simeon, a former MP who, along with his wife, had become Catholic, and who held that English Catholics could not be equal to fellow citizens unless something was done to improve their education. It was in vain to complain of the inferiority of their social position and, still worse, of their self-exclusion from society. Simeon pointed out the defects of Catholic colleges vis-à-vis public schools: the "want of manliness, want of completeness, want of definite purpose; and consequent want of influence on the future pursuits and character of man." He admired, however, their strengths: "the inculcation of purity and the consequent production of high moral standard."

Newman wished to educate the sons of his friends, most of

whom were converts. He wanted a Catholic Eton, offering students the best of the public schools while forming the students in virtue and religion. He inquired among friends about the financial support necessary to open such a school. At first the obstacle of competing against Catholic colleges seemed insurmountable. Those colleges, most of them seminaries which admitted lay students together with seminarians, each had the loyalty of old Catholic families.

Another one of Newman's friends, Edward Bellasis, concerned with the education of his eldest son, took it upon himself to sound out prospective parents and benefactors. Newman told him that the Oratory would be unable to support the school and after a number of years would relinquish its control. William Ullathorne, the Bishop of Birmingham, was sympathetic to the plan for a new school even though he came from an old Catholic family from York.

For Newman, the role of parents in the education of their children was of paramount importance, something that seems obvious but even to this day is not the case. Bellasis arranged meetings with seven promoters, all converts, interested in the establishment of the school. Newman relied significantly on their deliberation on many issues: including clarification of the role to be played by the Oratory, the social class origin of students sought, the source of funding, the cost to students, and location. In addition to Bellasis' leadership, Hope-Scott played a key role with his advice and financial support.

The discussions with the promoters led, among other points, to the choice of a location in the countryside, a fee that catered to upper classes but did not exclude a mixing of classes. More importantly, the goal sought was the establishment of the first Catholic public school. However, the desire to bring together Catholic morality and piety with the system of the English public schools would prove to be in practice very difficult, and a source of contention and division.

Shrimpton correctly points out that in this foundational period,

Newman was more cautious than he was in Dublin. He did not give lectures outlining his ideas, and, although he shared them with his closest friends, he waited for the deliberation and agreement of others. He was convinced of the need for the collaboration of parents as the first educators of their children.[3] Many years earlier, in 1826, he had preached on the purpose of education:

> Parents should consider that from the earliest infancy of their children they are their natural guardians and instructors; that sending to a school is merely an accidental circumstance, and but a part of education.[4]

Furthermore, Newman questioned the action of those satisfied that "they have done all that can be required of good and wise parents" when they have sent their children to school at the proper age. Parents must be responsible for the financial outlay of the school and for following up on the progress of their children, encouraging and correcting them as necessary, he said.

When the plan to start the school matured, Newman threw himself into the details. As before in Dublin, although on a different scale and now on his own ground, Newman made plans to procure space for the school and recruit teachers and students. The school was located on Hagley Road in Edgbaston, a growing suburb of Birmingham. The Edgbaston Catholic School opened in May 1859 with only seven students, all of them sons of converts. Classes were held in a building next to the Oratory adapted for classrooms, with a dormitory on the upper floor. Newman and some parents realized the need for the school to have a chapel, and they raised the money necessary to add one to the church that had been built for the Oratory in 1853. John Hungerford Pollen, who had designed the University Church in Dublin, designed the addition that was added to the existing church.[5]

---

[3] *A Catholic Eton?*, 84-85.

[4] "On popular mistakes as to the object of education," Sermon no. 128, *The Making of Men*, 85.

[5] Part of this church, the former St. Philip's Chapel, survives in a new church completed in 1909 for the Birmingham Oratory.

Although Newman was the founder, he chose Nicholas Darnell, a priest of the Oratory, as principal to run the school. Darnell, a former scholar at Winchester and fellow of New College, Oxford, had converted and joined the Oratory. He was an active, capable, and self-confident headmaster, but despite choosing him, Newman himself wished to act as president with overall control. He also chose young converts who were promising educators for the faculty.

Despite the very small number of initial students, the school got off to a good start and its enrollment grew since many families were drawn to the school because of Newman's association with it. The first students boarded with Mrs. Frances Wooten, widow of an Oxford doctor, in a three-story house, just a ten-minute walk from the Oratory. Mrs. Wooten, who had converted to Catholicism in 1850, moved to Birmingham to assist Newman. She became one of his most loyal friends and the main benefactress to the Oratory. The classes were on the first floor. In the mornings, Mass was celebrated by one of the Oratorians in a chapel on the top floor.

Newman understood that the care of children required the attention of women. They could best attend to their cleanliness, health and "superintendence of their childish weakness and troubles." Newman pursued this "dame system" employed at Eton, and also at the school at Ealing that he had attended. Mrs. Wooten took her duties seriously, caring for the children as a mother. When children were ill, she communicated with doctors and parents. She also kept accounts of the children's expenses and sent these to their parents. She did this so well and helped her charges to develop good habits and growth in virtue that Newman commented to a friend that she was "more like a Saint than most people you come across."[6] He thought that the system of dames or matrons made a very big contribution to the education of children. Since Mrs. Wooten was a lady of independent means, she

---

[6] JHN to Mrs. F. R. Ward (August 8, 1859), *LD*, Vol. 19: 188.

acted out of dedication for the children; the other ladies who later worked at the school did likewise.

In the second semester, the number of students grew to fourteen, and some of the newcomers were sons of old Catholics. By 1860, thirty-six boys were enrolled. A year later, two houses were converted for school use and construction of a new school building began. Not all parents agreed, and some were upset by the decision, believing a school in the countryside to be the best place for a boys' school and one independent from the Oratory. In keeping with the tradition of public schools, it was thought that school in the countryside would give the boys fresh air and keep them away from the dangers inherent in cities.

The guiding principles for the school were in some sense simple and based on knowledge of youth and common sense. They made up a vision of education similar to that of a university education, which consisted in the forming of a philosophical habit of mind, albeit adapted to a child's age, and the forging of his character. Newman articulated this vision in his conversations and correspondence with parents and faculty. His wisdom and experience inspired his friends, who were the parents of the students.

Personal freedom and responsibility constituted the foundation for the education of the boys. The boys had guidance, but they were not closely supervised as in seminaries or spied upon. As in the public schools, their freedom was respected, yet a moral sense of duty was equally instilled and discipline was maintained. This called for close collaboration with parents, which can be attested to by the numerous letters between Newman, Mrs. Wooten, and parents.

A select group of Oxford graduates imparted a classical education in the liberal arts to the students. In addition to Darnell, Newman chose masters to teach the students. One of these was Robert Mood, another convert who had been educated at Eton and Christ Church, Oxford. Mood moved to Edgbaston with his family and was allowed to take in boarders. Newman also enlisted Gerard Manley Hopkins, later a renowned poet, whom he had received years earlier at Oxford into the Catholic Church. The masters were assisted by tutors who were in charge of the character formation of the boys.

Among the students were Henry Fitzalan-Howard, fifteenth Duke of Norfolk, Augustine Scott-Murray, John Stokes, and Richard and Henry L. Bellasis. The most notable student was Hilaire Belloc, later a prolific writer who wrote of the school:

> They (the boys) were taught to be free—as self-reliant and as free—as any young Englishmen who were growing up around them in the great public schools; but with it all there an atmosphere of healthy religion, an unconstrained frequency in approaching Sacraments, a sincere faith and high code both of morals and of honour, which appeared so natural and so native to the place, that it would have been called spontaneous by anyone who did not know that the founding of the school, its influence, and its spirit were due to Cardinal Newman.[7]

Newman had in mind for two other Oratory fathers to be available for the confession and spiritual direction of the boys. The priests were supposed to prepare the children for the sacraments and lead them in devotions. Besides attendance at daily Mass, recitation of the Rosary before dinner and a visit to the Blessed Sacrament were part of the schedule. Under Fr. Darnell, however, the spiritual care and religious instruction of the boys was deficient. This improved considerably after he left the school.

Still from the start, the school was Catholic in its vision and practice. But it was not meant to be a seminary; it was a school for lay boys. When Bellasis thought that his eight-year old boy showed signs of a vocation to the priesthood, he was advised by a bishop to send him to one of the Catholic colleges. He also consulted Newman, who replied to him that true vocations are not destroyed by contact with the world. He explained that many boys

---

[7] "John Henry Cardinal Newman," *The Lamp* (1890), 39: 138-139, quoted in *A Catholic Eton?*, 284-285.

who seemed to show signs of an early calling later lost it because they never had a true vocation while others—for example, the saints—had received a vocation when they were young, which matured during the course of secular training.

Newman wrote Bellasis that the danger of the Church was not

(. . .) losing priests whom she ought to have had, but gaining priests she never should have been burdened with. The thought is awful, that boys should have had no trial of their hearts, till at the end of some 14 years, they go out into the world with the most solemn vows upon them, and then perhaps for the first time learn that the world is not a seminary.[8]

Bellasis decided to send his boy to join his older brother at the school. In the end, the older brother who had shown no signs of vocation became an Oratorian, while the younger one became a lawyer.

The school faced its first crisis in 1861, owing to the fact that it had begun with lax discipline under Darnell, who disregarded Newman's advice on this and other matters. After hearing of complaints, Newman composed some rules of conduct for the dormitories. However, Newman, unlike Darnell, was not aware that some students gambled and smoked. Over time a rift developed between Darnell, who wished to exercise complete control of the school, and Mrs. Wooten, who sided with Newman's policies and his plan that each have authority in their respective roles. Eventually Darnell resigned from the school and also left the Oratory despite Newman's entreaties. As a result some students were lost to the school and the confidence of parents, shaken. Newman suffered greatly from this turn of events and on medical advice was obliged to take a vacation.

The school, numbering fifty-six boys in December of 1861, survived the storm, again with the help of Bellasis and Hope-Scott. The latter advised Newman to become fully involved in the school business, a role he had left for the headmaster. New masters were

---

[8] JHN to Edward Bellasis, (August 5, 1861), *LD*, Vol. 20: 21.

hired. Richard Pope, a married convert, turned out to be an excellent appointment and held his post for thirty-eight years. Another convert was Thomas Arnold, the son of the famous headmaster of Rugby, then professor of English Literature of the Catholic University. The following year Newman's loyal friend, Ambrose St. John, once a pupil at Westminster School and later a fellow at Christ Church, Oxford, became the headmaster.

Parents had sent their children to the school because of Newman's reputation, and he was responsible for its success even though, as he claimed, the system of dames and the good care of Mrs. Wooten and other women had contributed greatly. His original choice of Fr. Darnell as headmaster, and slowness in exerting his authority over him, had been detrimental to the school. Hope-Scott, however, considered the crisis as a normal part of a nascent institution and an occasion to learn some lessons from it. As a result of the crisis, the relationship of the Oratory to the school was clarified, and from then on the name of the school changed to the Oratory School.

Following the advice of his friends, Newman shaped the Oratory School during the decade after the crisis, and it is during this same period that he made a personal contribution to secondary education.[9] Shrimpton elaborates on this contribution with many details, beginning with the fact that Newman never attended an English public school. His father had wanted him to go from the Ealing School, a private boarding school, on to Winchester, a recognized public school, but Newman remained at the Ealing School until the age of fifteen where he benefited from good teachers, small classes, first-rate facilities, and a healthy home environment. In addition to excelling in his studies, he acted in Latin plays, participated in debates, learned to play the violin, led a society for boys, and edited various school magazines. It was from this rich experience that Newman drew for his work in education.

Newman's affection for the students was evident; he loved them

9 See *A Catholic Eton?*, 169.

and enjoyed being with them, even though during the first years of the school he only saw the boys at Sunday Mass at the Oratory. Newman had grown old with the years and the many concerns that weighed on him. To the students he seemed like an old man whom they respected and remembered when looking back on their youth. He showed personal interest in each student because, for him, a school like a university was "an Alma Mater, knowing her children one by one, not a foundry, or a mint, or a treadmill."[10]

As a good educator, Newman encouraged parents to be patient with their children, to give them time to grow and go through normal childhood phases. He observed that boys developed their talents at different times, sometimes without having had success at school or shown signs of promise in a given field. He got to know the students well and was a good judge of their character. Every term, after the exams, he introduced the custom of giving students an account of their behavior and progress termed "characters." The students would have an interview with Newman, who would give them some words of encouragement or remonstrance.[11]

At the Oratory School, the curriculum was broader than the classics-based curriculum of the public schools, even though study of the classics was central, with Latin and Greek grammar, and mathematics to a lesser extent, occupying a major place in the education—because these help to form in the mind of youths the necessary idea of science, order, method, principle and system. In the *Idea of a University*, a book very well received by the masters at Eton, he had espoused the need to form a philosophical habit of mind in the youth.[12]

In contrast to l'Abbé Gaume, who at the time started a controversy in France in which he argued for replacing pagan authors with Christian ones, Newman held in the *Idea of a University* that the Church does not aim to exclude literature, "she fears no

---

[10] *Idea*, 144-145.

[11] *A Catholic Eton?*, 190.

[12] Shrimpton notes that Newman did not think that the natural sciences were sufficiently developed to serve as "a suitable training-ground for the intellect at a school level." *A Catholic Eton?*, 172

knowledge, but she purifies all; she represses no element of our nature, but cultivates the whole."[13] This required making a selection from classical authors, which was done at the Oratory School. Unlike the Catholic colleges where preference was given to the church fathers, emphasis was on classical authors who were used extensively. Besides the selection of texts, the expurgation of immoral and lewd parts was necessary. Newman objected to harmful thoughts introduced to the students by the reading of Lucretius, Plautus, and Terence.

As would be expected, given the school's aim at scholarship, a library was established in 1864. It had senior and junior sections and a librarian with three assistants. Newman drew up rules for the library and a list of fines. The library encouraged study; Newman was opposed to cramming for exams and superficial learning. As noted earlier, he gave importance to their examinations, sitting in on them. He also began the custom of an annual school play, organizing the performance of classical plays, which he edited to remove any morally harmful scenes. For him the performances of plays, like the examinations, were highly formative and thus deserved careful attention.

Not surprisingly, under Fr. Ambrose St. John and with Newman's guidance, religious instruction and piety gained their proper place at the school. The schedule of religious acts was now carefully observed, beginning with morning prayers at 6:50 a.m. followed by Mass at 7:00 a.m., and prayer of the Angelus at noon. At night before retiring, there were evening prayers and spiritual reading, followed by a few minutes for private prayers. During Holy Week, all the students attended a three-day spiritual retreat.

The Sacrament of Confession was given the importance it deserves. John Walford, who had taught at Harrow and Eton, wrote a friend that he was impressed by

> (. . .) the manliness of the Edgbaston boys and the fervent piety of many, the combination not having been frequent in his previous experience. The bearing of the Sacrament of Pen-

[13] *Idea*, 233-234.

ance, not only on individual souls, but on the discipline and purity of school life, came to him like a revelation.[14]

Of equal importance was the respect and freedom afforded the students in religious practices. An example of this was attendance at the prayer of the Rosary, which was optional. Newman offered the boys other devotions throughout the year, such as the Stations of the Cross on Fridays in Lent, Marian devotions in May, a Corpus Christi procession, and a novena for St. Philip's feast day. In the devotions as well as in religious instructions, Newman had in mind, as noted earlier, the masculine nature of the boys and the need to capture their imaginations.

He also understood their need for recreation and sports. The boys played hockey, football, and croquet, and also went out for walks. The school had a pavilion for cricket matches and a billiard room for the older boys. Major feast days were singled out, with holidays celebrated with High Mass, followed by festive meals. Starting in 1865, on the days leading up to the feast of St. Philip, there were three performances of the annual Latin play.

This account of Newman's work as an educator reveals many elements that he held important in education and which were a continuation of his earlier work as tutor at Oriel College, Oxford, and later founder of the Catholic University of Ireland—elements such as the need for a liberal arts education, personal guidance of students, formation of their moral character, and religious practices. In this his third and last work in education, he demonstrated the invaluable role of parents and laity in the foundation and running of a school, and how the intellectual and the moral and religious formation could be integrated in the education of boys. Although the scope of the project was considerably smaller than that of the university, it, too, was very demanding and faced many difficulties. Under his direct attention and control and that of the Oratory, he was able to fully engage parents and laity to make the school successful, something he had not be able to do in Dublin.

---

[14] Quoted in *A Catholic Eton?*, 181.

Fourteen

FAITH, REASON, AND SCIENCE

To speak of faith and reason seems to return to a worn-out and hopeless subject; yet at no time more than in recent decades have people discussed a supposed controversy between faith and reason. Faith has become synonymous with soft thinking, and reason with science. Newman faced this problem in English thought in the second half of the twentieth century and offered some valuable insights.

Ever since the birth of science in ancient Greece, men have questioned the gods. Man wishes to know how things work and why. He wishes to know the cause of things, and when he questions this, he also questions the ultimate cause of things—the Creator himself. Science gives an account of the world based on reason, whereas faith gives an account of causes beyond the material world.

Already in ancient Greece, a few thinkers put into doubt the need for explanations based on faith and religion. All philosophers sought the elements that make up the world, but there were some, whom we would call materialists, who thought that matter alone explains itself. Their way of reasoning became more pronounced with the rise of the Enlightenment and nineteenth-century scientific discoveries. It was not always the case, beginning with Plato and Aristotle, who postulated non-material principles in the causation of things. Through the early Middle Ages, thinkers acknowledged this non-material or spiritual principle called the soul and God, its maker.

St. Thomas Aquinas, who subscribed to St. Anselm's idea of faith seeking understanding (*fides quaerens intellectum*), saw a harmony between faith and reason. As we discussed in an earlier chapter, this important relationship began to suffer with Roger Bacon, Isaac Newton, and Galileo Galilei, and at last ruptured with René Descartes, David Hume, and John Locke.[1]

In a period of English history that saw the rise of agnosticism as well as scientific societies, John Henry Newman put forth ideas, especially in his *Idea of a University*, that defend and favor a healthy relationship between faith and reason, and between religion and science as Paschal had done in Descartes' age.[2] For the second centenary of Newman's birth, Pope John Paul II wrote:

> Rationalism brought with it a rejection of both authority and transcendence, while fideism turned from the challenges of history and the tasks of this world to a distorted dependence upon authority and the supernatural. In such a world, Newman came eventually to a *remarkable synthesis of faith and reason* which were for him "like two wings on which the human spirit rises to the contemplation of the truth" (*Fides et ratio*, Introduction; cf. *ibid.*, 74).[3]

Newman put forth various ways in which, through reason alone, man can come to the natural knowledge of God. These consist in the argument from moral conscience, the argument from desire or yearning for God, and, to a lesser degree, the arguments from design and from causality. In the *Grammar of Assent*, he described how the moral conscience develops in a child and informs him of a Judge who is all-powerful. The child later realizes that a Judge implies a Lawmaker and that God is both a Judge and Lawmaker. As Ian Ker notes, however, in the novel *Callista* (1855), Newman pointed to another argument, the sense of unfulfillment and de-

---

[1] Newman criticized points of David Hume's philosophy and that of John Locke in his *Grammar of Assent*, 45, 78, 293, and 151-153, 164, 166, 288, 304 respectively. In addition to his philosophical denial of causation, Hume rejected and ridiculed the Christian belief in miracles.

[2] It is worthwhile noting that although Newman was not a mathematician like Paschal, he also studied physics and appreciated astronomy while at Oxford.

[3] John Paul II, Letter on the Occasion of the 2nd Centenary of the Birth of Cardinal John Henry Newman (January 22, 2001). Vatican website: http://w2.vatican.va/content/john-paul-ii/en/letters/2001/documents/hf_jp-ii_let_20010227_john-henry-newman.html.

sire for happiness: ultimately the yearning for God. The young Greek woman in the novel does not ask herself about right and wrong. When she speaks with Bishop Caecilius, the fictitious name Newman gave to St. Cyprian, the Bishop of Carthage tells her of the happiness that lasts, which is heaven, whereas hell is a kind of self-imprisonment. Then he argues that the soul needs an object upon which to rest.[4]

The Bishop of Carthage asks the young Greek to make an imaginative leap concerning the object of which the soul has a presentiment and which is the remedy for all human desires, aims, and aspirations. The bishop tells Callista:

Every man is in that state in which you confess yourself. We have not love for Him who alone lasts. We love those things which do not last, but come to an end. Things being thus, He whom we ought to love has determined to win us back to Him. With this object He has come into His own world, in the form of one of us men. And in the human form He opens His arms and woos us to return to Him, our Maker. This is our Worship, this is our Love, Callista.[5]

Ker points out that Callista's conversion is not, however, complete. She needs to have a clearer image of the Christ that is in her imagination. She must encounter the figure of the Christ found in the Gospels and reach a personal love for the Object of Faith. Then, reading a manuscript of St. Luke's Gospel that Caecilius had given to her, she experiences the second stage of her conversion. She reads it, remembering words the bishop had told her: "Here you will see who it is we love (. . .)" and Newman explains:

Here was that to which her intellect tended, though that intellect could not frame it. It could approve and acknowledge, when set before it, what it could not originate. Here was He who spoke to her in her conscience; whose Voice she heard,

[4] Ian Ker, "John Henry Newman: Analogy, Image and Reality," *Newman Studies Journal*, Vol. 12, Number 2 (Fall 2015), 15-32.
[5] John Henry Newman, *Callista: A Tale of the Third Century*, [1855/1888], (London: Longmans, Green, and Co., 1901), 221.

whose Person she was seeking for (. . .) That image sank deep into her; she felt it to be a reality.

Natural religion based on reason alone is insufficient. The created world speaks only of the perfection and beauty of an all-perfect and all-beautiful Creator. Revelation affirms arguments of design and causality, but it does much more: it brings man before the Living God, the personal God who became incarnate in Jesus Christ. With the Church's Tradition, Newman thus spoke of a supernatural knowledge of God which comes to man through God's own revelation of himself.

The testimony of the early Christians and the growth of the Church are also powerful arguments for the Christian truths about God. Only a supernatural explanation can account for the fortitude of the Christian martyrs and the rapid spread of Christianity. Newman devoted a good number of pages to the moving narrative of some of the martyrs' deaths.

Contemporary fundamental theology takes the important step forward of seeing in the person of Jesus Christ and his teaching the primary argument for God's existence. This, however, does not invalidate the arguments that many, including Newman, have advanced over the centuries and that often serve as a preparation for arguments from revelation.

For Newman, man reaches certitude about his knowledge of God through what he names the *illative sense*. He believed this type of knowledge consists in the confluence of many impressions, experiences, and thoughts that leads a person to conclusions and provides certainty. It is akin to the knowledge gained from taking one or several looks at a painting. He offered the analogy of a cable made up of many threads: "The best illustration (. . .) is that of a *cable* which is made up of a number of separate threads, each feeble, yet together as sufficient as an iron rod."[6] He was improving on Keble's version of Bishop Butler's dictum that 'probability is the guide of life.'[7]

---

[6] JHN to John Walker of Scarborough, (July 6, 1864), *LD*, Vol. 21:146.
[7] For a good exposition of religious belief according to Newman, see Ker, 618-623.

A person arrives at the knowledge of God and other truths all at once without a discursive process or at least a conscious inductive or deductive process. According to him, the person, mind and heart, knows God and reality without following a process of formal logic. Syllogisms cannot account for many things that we know, and cannot provide the mind with the necessary certitude. The latter is not the assent to a conclusion; rather it is the result of an *assemblage* of concurring and converging probabilities.[8] For him certitude is the unconditional recognition of a belief as truth.

Just as Newman respected the operation of the mind in the knowledge of God, he respected the workings of empirical sciences. He did not think that belief in God and the Christian doctrine of creation was contradicted by findings of modern science. In keeping with the principle of the circle of knowledge in a university, and the proper autonomy of the sciences, he was not alarmed by the observations Charles Darwin made in his *Origin of Species*. Along the same line as St. Augustine, he taught that the Bible is not a book on natural sciences even though through it, we learn of the beliefs and modes of expressions of the human authors and their times. The Scriptures narrate salvation history. That is their purpose—not to prove or disprove scientific explanations.

Newman was in fact open to Darwin's scientific ideas, expressing his thoughts in a letter to a clergyman who sent him a book by Robert Beverley advocating the argument from design.

> I do not fear the theory [of evolution] so much as he [Beverly] seems to do—and it seems to me that he is hard upon Darwin sometimes, which (sic) he might have interpreted him kindly. It does not seem to me to follow that creation is denied because the Creator, millions of years ago, gave laws to matter. He first created matter and then he created laws for it—laws which should *construct* it into its present wonderful beauty, and accurate adjustment and harmony of parts *gradually*.[9]

[8] See *Apo.*, 30-31.
[9] JHN to John Walker of Scarborough, (May 22, 1868), *LD*, Vol. 24: 77-78.

Newman was possibly predisposed to Darwin's ideas because he rejected the natural theology of William Paley.[10] In his *Natural Theology or Evidences of the Existence and Attributes of the Deity* (1802) Paley attempted to prove the existence of God and the moral order based on the Enlightenment notion of God as a watchmaker. Newman felt that according to this view, God cannot act in his creation; he is identified with it. He wrote: "Indeed a Being of Power, Wisdom, and Goodness, and nothing else, is not very different from the God of the Pantheist."[11] For Newman, Darwin's theory, which may or not be true in all its parts, presupposed the existence of a Creator and in itself it was not incompatible with the Christian faith.

Christianity and Scientific Investigation

In a lecture to the School of Sciences at the Catholic University, he compared the university to the old Roman Empire with a hundred different peoples, each with its privileged and legitimate range of action. A university, he explains,

> (. . .) maps out the territory of the intellect, and sees that the boundaries of each province are religiously respected, and that there is neither encroachment nor surrender on any side. It acts as umpire between truth and truth, and, taking into account the nature and importance of each, assigns to all their due order of precedence.[12]

Newman felt that the various professors were like the ministers of various political powers at court. Pursuing the analogy, he called the university an "imperial intellect" with its philosophy to take in all sciences that reflect the human intellect, and to "live and let live." For him a university recognizes the lines of demarcation between subjects, how truths lie relative to one other, where they concur and where they part company. The representative of a uni-

[10] Ryan Vilbig, "John Henry Newman's view of the 'Darwin Theory'," *Newman Studies Journal*, Vol. 8, Number 2 (Fall 2011), 52-61.
[11] *Idea*, 454.
[12] John Henry Newman, "Christianity and Scientific Investigation" in *Idea*, 345.

versity must recognize the real and apparent difficulties, some allowing a rational skepticism and others claiming a peremptory faith.

Newman went on to offer valuable advice to any head of a university:

> If he has one cardinal maxim in his philosophy, it is, that truth cannot be contrary to truth; if he has a second, it is, that truth often *seems* contrary to truth; and, if a third, it is the practical conclusion, that we must be patient with such appearances, and not be hasty to pronounce them to be really of a more formidable character.[13]

Newman provided examples in the natural order of extreme contrariety of ideas in physics regarding space and time, and in mathematics. For instance, we cannot deny the existence of space, yet we find it impossible that it comes to a limit anywhere. Newman argued that, if we are patient when finding such difficulties in the sciences, we must also be patient when finding difficulties between sciences and religious truths. In his words:

> (. . .) so you should not think it very hard to be told that there exists, here and there, not an inextricable difficulty, not an astounding contrariety, not (much less) a contradiction as to clear facts between Revelation and Nature; but a hitch, an obscurity, a divergence of tendency, a temporary antagonism, a difference of tone, between the two—that is, between Catholic opinion on the one hand, and astronomy, or geology, or physiology, or ethnology, or political economy, or history, or antiquities, on the other.[14]

Newman begged both scientists and theologians "to keep the peace, to live in good will, and to exercise equanimity"[15] when apparent discrepancies exist between truths of nature and truths of revelation, confident that one day they will ultimately be re-

---

[13] *Idea*, 347.
[14] *Idea*, 350.
[15] *Idea*, 350.

solved. Again this advice applies to university studies and research today.

Based on this confidence that requires patience and mutual respect, Newman made a bold declaration about the pursuit of scientific truths: Catholics are not afraid of science; they are not afraid of the truth.

> I say, then, he who believes Revelation with the absolute faith which is the prerogative of a Catholic, is not the nervous creature who startles at every sudden sound, and is fluttered by every strange or novel appearance which meets his eyes. He has no sort of apprehension, he laughs at the idea, that any thing can be discovered by any other scientific method, which can contradict any one of the dogmas of his religion.[16]

Once more Newman provided very good advice to students and researchers explaining the reason for this confidence:

> [A Catholic] is sure, and nothing shall make him doubt, that, if anything seems to be proved by astronomer, or geologist, or chronologist, or antiquarian, or ethnologist, in contradiction to the dogmas of faith, that point will eventually turn out, first *not* to be proved, or secondly, not *contradictory*, or thirdly, not contradictory to any thing *really revealed*, but to something which has been confused with revelation.[17]

By way of example, Newman referred to the time when the Copernican system gained acceptance. Some thought that this contradicted the Church's teaching and authoritative interpretation of Scripture. But on more careful examination this was not the case. The Church has never made formal pronouncements on cosmology, nor will it; that is the purview of astronomy. Nor did the Church proscribe intellectual activity. On the contrary, she fostered it, as can be seen in the age of the universities when there was a vigorous exercise of reason, and debate in theological matters.

---

[16] *Idea*, 351.
[17] *Idea.*, 351.

Despite its temporal power during the Middle Ages, the Church, according to Newman, did not take a high hand against the philosophy of Aristotle, which presented apparent contradictions with Christianity, and for which the early church fathers had shown aversion. She allowed a spirit of free inquiry and debate. Although the Bishop of Paris censured many propositions of St. Thomas Aquinas' philosophy because of his reliance on Aristotle, the Church vindicated Aquinas and never denounced Aristotle. In the end, St. Thomas Aquinas "made him a hewer of wood and drawer of water to the Church. A strong slave he is; and the Church herself has given her sanction to the use in Theology of the ideas and terms of his philosophy."[18]

For its part, the progress of science requires free discussion, and Newman told the students that, in science, investigators should be free and without impediments in their research as long as they respected moral principles and dogmas of faith. Galileo's error was precisely to propose his "philosophical or historical conclusions as the formal interpretation of the sacred text."[19] According to Newman, he should have held to his "doctrine of the motion of the earth as a scientific conclusion (. . .) leaving it to those whom it really concerned to compare it with Scripture."[20]

Newman thought that scientists should also avoid scandalizing the weak by reckless speculation that shocked the popular mind. At the same time he warned religious men from accommodating biblical explanations to geological or other scientific propositions, having to change them just as soon as it became necessary from other developments in science. Newman advised patience with what we feel to be error. He noted that scientific research takes many stages and is the work of many minds, with some continuing where others have left off. "There are no short cuts to knowledge; nor does the road to it always lie in the direction in which it terminates, nor are we able to see the end on starting."[21] Likewise

[18] *Idea*, 354.
[19] *Idea*, 355.
[20] *Idea*, 355.
[21] *Idea*, 357.

"no one can go straight up a mountain; no sailing vessel makes for its port without tacking."[22]

Today more than ever, science and faith seem like worlds apart. Yet, they have two objects in common: man and the world, although they study them from very different vantage points. At our present crossroads, Newman's advice, of great importance to both sides, is to accord each other mutual respect and to be patient in the resolution of apparent contradictions.

In light of this exhortation to respect a field of knowledge in its own sphere, the sciences are called upon to acknowledge the fundamental requirements of ethics and moral theology that uphold the dignity of every human being. Biomedical research, in particular, should treat procreation, the human fetus, the elderly, and research subjects with the respect claimed by the Catholic Church.

In addition to expounding on the rights and duties of scientists and theologians, Newman corrected the erroneous notion that faith and the Catholic Church are inimical to science and progress. Lastly, while he presented various arguments based on reason for the existence of God, he indicated the need for a personal knowledge of Christ through faith.

---

[22] *Idea*, 357.

Fifteen

ECCLESIOLOGY AND CONVERTS

The history of the Church shows an important renewed awareness of the need for Christian unity and a significant effort to achieve it in the twentieth century. Newman made a small contribution to the roots of this ecumenical movement dating in modern times back to the second quarter of the nineteenth century. Here we wish to consider how Newman understood the divisions among Christians and what he thought was the duty of a Christian in the face of these divisions.

To begin, we must acknowledge that Christ knew that there would be divisions among Christians. On the night of the Last Supper, he earnestly prayed to the Father for their unity. Over the centuries there have been many sad divisions among Christians; major ones occurred in the fourth century with the Arians, in the eleventh century with the Orthodox, and in the sixteenth century with the Protestants. Christ's desire and prayer resulted in various attempts at reunification, especially between the Sees of Rome and Constantinople at various ecumenical councils. During the second half of the nineteenth century, a renewed desire for Christian unity arose, especially in England and the United States through the work of Fr. George Spencer.[1]

Fr. Spencer, a Roman Catholic priest, visited Oxford, asking Newman and others to join him in a prayer campaign for the

---

[1] Years later, in 1908, Fr. Paul James Wattson, an Episcopalian clergyman in New York State, began to observe eight days of prayer for this intention between the Feast of the Chair of Peter, then celebrated on January 18 and the Feast of the Conversion of St. Paul, January 25, to pray for the unity of Christians.

unity of Christians. Manning and Pusey wrote Newman that Anglicans already prayed in their daily services for those in the "Catholic Church," whereas Roman Catholics prayed only once a year (on Good Friday) for the Anglicans together with other heretics. To this Newman retorted that many Anglicans did not actually pray for Roman Catholics but instead reviled them. He added that if Roman Catholics practiced duplicity, they needed all the more the prayers of Anglicans.

Newman, too, would pray for the unity of Christians, but at first as a young Anglican clergyman he focused on the history of the divisions in early Church history. His first book, titled *The Arians of the Fourth Century* (1833), examined the Christological controversies—the protagonist and the Church councils convened to settle matters. For him, as was habitual in his time, the errors put forth by bishops and other religious leaders were called heresies. He pursued the study of these early heresies with an eye to understand doctrinal errors of his own time, and to draw lessons from them.

At that period in the development of his own religious convictions, Newman adhered to the Branch Theory of Christianity whereby the Anglican, Orthodox, and Roman Catholic churches were three branches of the same one Church founded by Jesus Christ. This notion did not address the all-important question of doctrinal unity and ecclesial authority. It was no more than a well-intentioned yet vague notion of spiritual unity, or desire for that unity.

The emptiness of this notion became all too evident as the Oxford Movement sought to revive ecclesial discipline, doctrinal purity, and earlier liturgical and sacramental practices. As noted earlier in this book, Newman had come up with a paper idea of the Anglican Church as a *via media* between Protestantism and Roman Catholicism, but this, too, turned out to be unrealistic. The consideration of the fourth century Arian heresy made Newman realize that Anglicans were not in fact a good middle way or *via media*; the truth lay with the Roman Catholics at one end and, instead, they were in the middle like the semi-Arians.[2]

In his preaching, Newman spoke of the one fold of Christ, referring to Jesus' teaching about the Good Shepherd. The sheep pertain to one fold; they hear the voice of the shepherd, and they go in and out the gate in reply to his voice. Jesus speaks of other sheep that are not of the fold but who also need to hear his voice. Study of Church history and the church fathers led him to recognize the "notes" of the Church of which the fathers spoke: antiquity, catholicity, apostolicity, and holiness. Being an Anglican, he naturally sought evidence that the Anglican Church had these "notes". Over time he could not fail to see that the Anglicans, like the Donatists,, had gone outside the communion of the Church and thus were lacking in *catholicity*. Given the increase of doctrinal dissent and confusion among Anglicans, he grasped for justification for his adherence to the Anglican Church. For a short time he found it in the idea that the Anglicans had the note of holiness, which for a while he thought Roman Catholics lacked as a whole, and the sense that he should remain where God had placed him.

On one occasion he awoke and saw himself as in a mirror to be outside of the Catholic Church; the thought of St. Athanasius or St. Jerome coming to life from the tomb and disowning the Anglican Church was also present in his mind. Thus, the consideration of the "notes" of the Church moved Newman to believe that the fullness of faith was only present in the Church of Rome, and he began a long period of discernment about joining the Roman Catholic Church. It was during this period that Fr. Spencer asked Newman to pray for the unity of Christian communities. At first Newman was reticent to acquiesce to common prayer for this intention because of Irish Catholic support of political agitators in

---

[2] In 1841, while studying once more St. Athanasius and the Arian Heresy, Newman was gripped again by the thought he first had in 1839. He realized that the Arians were equivalent to the Protestants; the semi-Arians were like the Anglicans, and Rome held the position she had always had. "The truth lay, not with the *Via Media*, but with what was called 'the extreme party.'" *Apo.*, 139.

Ireland, but he later agreed to promote prayer for this unity and circulated a draft of a prayer to be said by Anglicans.

Feeling the constant scrutiny of the public eye, Newman felt great responsibility not to mislead men to the Catholic Church, men who looked up to him as an Anglican clergyman. Some junior men at Oxford said, "I will go if N. goes," or "Would you go over if K. and N. did?"[3] Some friends asked him questions about future events, something Newman did not yet wish to consider. At the start of 1841, he wrote his friend Henry Wilberforce, who was contemplating conversion to Roman Catholicism, "*How long do you want before you turn R. C.? will two years do? Let me know this important point.*"[4] Toward the end of 1841, following the condemnation of *Tract* 90 and other significant events, Newman then told various friends, including Henry Wilberforce, that he did not discard the possibility of one day going over to Rome, but it would not be a sudden move.[5] Even then Newman was concerned with countering the rumor that he and others were seceding to Rome.[6]

The events that followed, leading to Newman's acceptance of full communion with the Roman Catholic Church on October 9, 1845, are narrated in different biographies. Here I wish to point out the advice that Newman gave to people who sought his counsel on pursuing the same course. Through the impetus of the Oxford Movement, and especially through Newman's preaching and example, many Anglicans converted to the Roman Catholic Church. Some of these converts knew him personally or had heard him preach; many others had read his sermons.

Individual Conversions

Newman told those who sought his advice that they should follow a period of discernment over a number of years, no less than three,

---

[3] JHN to Henry Wilberforce (November 8, 1841), *LD*, Vol. 8: 320-322; 322. "K." refers to John Keble, and "N." to Newman.

[4] JHN to Henry William Wilberforce (March 1, 1841), *LD*, Vol. 8: 45-46; 46.

[5] JHN to Henry Wilberforce (November 8, 1841), *LD*, Vol. 8: 320-22; 321.

[6] JHN to Mrs. J. Mozley (November 16, 1841), *LD*, Vol. 8: 334-35; 334.

lest the person should make a hasty decision based on sentimental motives or poor reasoning. This was the advice to his brother-in-law Thomas Mozley, who in the end never joined the Catholic Church. Some did wait and then took the same step as he did; and others, such as Ms. Mary Holmes, joined without heeding his advice. Newman had tried to dissuade her by telling her that one should not act on first inspirations but should instead think and pray about God's will. He counseled her: "To any friend who asked me what to do, I should prescribe three years, during which his thoughts and prayers should be directed this one way, to learn God's will."[7] A person who wished to become Roman Catholic should, according to Newman, pray and wait for God's grace, without impatience or hasty decisions. This is what he did in his own case.

To Newman, such an important decision as renouncing one's membership in a religious body required a calm period of study and prayer. He warned people against private judgment in these matters, suggesting that persons not only mature in their decisions but move as a group rather than individually. Newman knew of people who had become Roman Catholic only later to leave that Church and in some cases return to the Anglican Church. He had retired to Littlemore for this very reason: to study and to pray. It was there that he studied the difficulties he found in Catholic doctrine and practices, the fruit of which was *An Essay on the Development of Christian Doctrine*. Prayer of the Roman breviary and personal meditation allowed him to grow in appreciation and understanding of the truths that he studied.

In an almost imperceptible way, grace acted in Newman's soul and gradually opened the door for him to Rome. There were external events, especially the condemnation of *Tract* 90 by the Anglican Bishops, that affected Newman, but he did not act impulsively. He remained in the Anglican Communion for a few more years until, gradually, he began to sense God's voice in his conscience telling him that he must become a Roman Catholic. Over

---

[7] JHN to Miss Holmes (August 8, 1841), *LD*, Vol. 8: 238-39.

time, this step became for him a matter of conscience.

A friend, Edward Coleridge, a clergyman and Master at Eton College, made an earnest appeal for him not to leave the Church of England unless he was absolutely obliged by conscience.[8] Coleridge argued that Newman's secession would have an effect on numerous people who relied implicitly on Newman's steps and would actually follow him, acting against their own consciences. Newman replied, "The pain that I feel at the distress I am causing others, at the great unsettlement of mind I am causing, and the ties I am rending, is keener than I can say."[9] Then Newman made a remarkable statement: that the only motive upon which he acted was a sense of duty, "imperative to my salvation."[10] Newman's intellectual reasoning had become a moral conviction. He felt obliged in conscience to act in obedience to a higher law for the sake of his salvation.

In 1850, some years after his conversion to Catholicism, New-man gave a series of lectures, later titled *Certain Difficulties Felt by Anglicans in Catholic Teaching*, which were intended to win con-verts to the Catholic faith. It is important to note that Newman addressed the lectures to educated people, many of whom were part of the Oxford Movement. He thought that they were in a good position to understand that the Roman Catholic Church is the one fold established by Christ and placed under a universal vicar. The goal of his lectures and natural end of the movement, he told Anglo-Catholics, was their full communion with Rome, that they "be lodged safely in the true home of your souls and the valley of peace."[11]

Newman did not incite to hasty conversions but sought to move hesitant friends such as Keble and Pusey to join him. Although the friendship among the three would be rekindled years later, these and other friends remained Anglicans all their lives. How-

[8] *LD*, Vol. 10: 399, footnote.
[9] JHN to Edward Coleridge (November 12, 1844), *LD*, Vol. 10: 398-99; 398.
[10] *LD*, Vol. 10, 399.
[11] *Diff.*, Vol. I: 360.

ever, in the aftermath of the so-called Gorham case and Newman's lectures, there was a wave of converts. Many of these came from Oxford and Cambridge graduates, aristocratic families and professionals. These included Henry Wilberforce, James Hope-Scott, and Edward Manning.

Ecumenism, Corporate Reunion

The Catholic Church does not discourage individual Christians, who after study and careful discernment of the Catholic faith, wish to enter into full communion with it, and every year, especially at Easter, she receives into her fold new members from other Christian communities. At the same time, however, her prayers for the unity of all these Christian communities increased in the twentieth century, and intensified further after Vatican II. As such, in the second half of the twentieth century, various popes worked extensively to restore this unity. A decisive advance in the cause for unity was made in 1965 with the revocation by Pope Paul VI and Patriarch Athenagoras of the mutual excommunications of Rome and Constantinople in the eleventh century.

During the second half of the twentieth century there were extensive and fruitful theological dialogues with representatives from different churches and ecclesial communities. The aim of ecumenism as described by the Vatican II decree *Unitatis Redintegratio* (1964) is the corporate reunion of Christians into one body. Pope John Paul II considered that Newman, who wrote "that the Church must be prepared for converts, as well as converts prepared for the Church:"[12]

> (. . .) already in a certain measure anticipated in his broad theological vision one of the main aims and orientations of the Second Vatican Council and the Church in the post-conciliar period.[13]

[12] *AW*, 258.
[13] Letter of John Paul II on the occasion of the Centenary of the Cardinalate of Cardinal John Henry Newman (April 7, 1979). *Newman Reader*: http://www.newmanreader.org/canonization/popes/or21may79.html

Newman lived in a period of English history in which there was widespread injustice and prejudice against Catholics. Despite the then only recent restoration of civil rights for Roman Catholics, the reestablishment of the Catholic hierarchy only took place in 1850. Justice and mutual respect would be necessary before any fruitful cooperation and eventual pursuit of unity would materialize.

Thus Newman did not think that a direct union between the Anglican Church and Rome would take place in his lifetime, but he advised a union of hearts and a focus on improving their own religious bodies respectively. Before his own conversion, he expressed the opinion that Tractarians had done a lot to improve the "English Communion." He thought, for example, that Ambrose Phillips, a convert from Anglicanism, who promoted the reunification of the Anglican and Catholic Churches, was a good example for the Roman Catholics, but that they should do much more. Newman urged that Roman Catholics live charity better, influence the tone of their publications, give up "uncatholic" things, such as using churches for music recitals, and preach sanctity and moral reformation.[14] He also argued that reunification was the prerogative of only those in authority, namely the bishops, and that the time was not yet ripe for it.

Some years before his conversion, Newman admitted to Phillips that in addition to the main obstacle to union, a political one, there were two important obstacles to unity: the Roman Catholic doctrine of Transubstantiation and devotion to Mary. He maintained that this Eucharistic doctrine and Marian piety were not found in early Christianity. Newman later retracted his position on the antiquity of devotion to Mary. Today, more than a century later, these and other doctrinal matters, such as the primacy of Peter's successor and the validity of priestly ordination, continue to pose serious difficulties in the ecumenical dialogue.

Although Newman did eventually convert—and advised the individual conversion of others who after necessary discernment

---

[14] Letter of John Paul II on the occasion of the Centenary of the Cardinalate of Cardinal John Henry Newman , 43.

were ready to do so—while an Anglican he opposed individual conversions in favor of corporate reunion. In a letter that he wrote but never sent to Nicholas Wiseman to explain his position, he insisted that Catholics should improve their tone, remove abuses, and conciliate Anglicans in word and deed. "Such conduct on both sides must tend eventually to unity, *in God's time*, though, it may be, not in our day."[15] Even though Newman changed his opposition to individual conversions, this way of thinking about ecumenical relations maintains the same validity today.

Once a Roman Catholic, Newman would understand how much the Anglicans had to do on their part. He then realized the depth and extent of prejudice and injustice against Catholics. In a series of lectures titled *On the Present Position of Catholics in England* (1851), we find his most sarcastic and humorous criticism of English bigotry against Catholics. He begins one lecture with the fable of a man and a lion, where the former represents the Church of England and the latter the Catholic religion. A man invited a lion to his magnificent palace with rich works of art, most of them showing lions hunted or killed. "There was a lion in a net; a lion in a trap; four lions, yoked in harness, were drawing the car of a Roman emperor; and elsewhere stood Hercules clad in a lion's skin, and with the club which demolished him."[16] When the host asked the guest what he thought of the mansion and its artwork, Newman writes that he did justice in replying, "Lions would have fared better, had lions been the artists."[17]

As Newman pointed out, prejudice is transmitted from one generation to another; it is almost inbred. Prejudice can be overcome through study and right reasoning, but in the end it requires meeting Christians of other confessions to discover its falsehood. In this vein, Newman's closing lecture offers worthy advice for the cause of Christian unity. In it he told his fellow Oratorians how their very lives would be the means through which bigotry would be overcome.

---

[15] JHN to Nicholas Wiseman (October 14, 1841), *LD, Vol. 8*: 297-98; 298. The letter was not sent.

[16] *Pres. Pos.*, 4.

[17] *Pres. Pos.*, 4.

You see, then, Brothers of the Oratory, where your success lies, and how you are to secure it. Never mind the London press; never mind Exeter Hall; never mind perambulating orators or solemn meetings: let them alone, they do not affect local opinion. They are a blaze amid the stubble; they glare, and they expire. Do not dream of converting the public opinion of London; you cannot, and you need not. Look at home, there lies your work; what you have to do, and what you can do, are one and the same. Prove to the people of Birmingham, as you can prove to them, that your priests and yourselves are not without conscience, or honour, or morality; prove it to them (. . .) You are your own best, and sure, and sufficient friends; no one can really hurt you but yourselves; no one can succour you but yourselves. Be content to have your conscience clear, and your God on your side.[18]

Each Christian is called to live a coherent life, to live what he preaches, and this is what turns people's minds and hearts. A century later the Vatican II documents echoed this truth, calling for a spiritual ecumenism based on charity and prayer. A change of heart and holiness of life, along with public and private prayer for the unity of Christians, should be regarded as the soul of the whole ecumenical movement, and can rightly be called 'spiritual ecumenism.'[19]

Some years later, Pope John Paul II, who worked tirelessly for the cause of Christian unity, underscored, as Newman had done, that love for truth must be accompanied with true humility and charity. In the encyclical *Ut Unum Sint* he wrote:

Love for the truth is the deepest dimension of any authentic quest for full communion between Christians. Without this love it would be impossible to face the objective theological, cultural, psychological and social difficulties which appear

[18] *Pres. Pos.*, 385, 388.
[19] See Second Vatican' Council's Decree on Ecumenism *Unitatis Redintegratio* (November 21, 1964), n. 8. Vatican website: www.vatican.va.

when disagreements are examined. This dimension, which is interior and personal, must be inseparably accompanied by a spirit of charity and humility. There must be charity towards one's partner in dialogue, and humility with regard to the truth which comes to light and which might require a review of assertions and attitudes.[20]

It would be interesting to speculate what more Newman could have done to promote a corporate reunion of Christian bodies. A good part of the last years of his life was fully dedicated to educational pursuits: first the Catholic University of Ireland and later the Oratory School, which, in addition to his duties as the head of the Birmingham Oratory, kept him fully occupied. Furthermore, and perhaps more importantly, Newman was not in a position to promote or participate in dialogues between representatives of the Anglican and Roman Catholic hierarchies, a requisite for corporate reunion.

When his Anglican friend Pusey wrote to him in 1866 about two interviews with the Catholic Archbishop of Paris on the subject of corporate reunion, Newman showed interest and gave his encouragement, but he was not part of this interview or similar ones. For his part, along with the insights he expressed with regard to Christian unity, he joined the centuries-old prayer for this cause revived in Europe by Fr. Spencer and afterwards by others including Fr. Paul J. Wattson, Abbé Paul Couturier, Abbess Maria Pia, and Mother Maria Gabriella.[21]

---

[20] John Paul II, Encyclical letter *Ut Unum Sint*, (May 25, 1995), n. 36. Vatican website: www.vatican.va.

[21] In 1933, a French priest, Abbé Paul Couturier, extended the octave of prayer to those who sought a spiritual ecumenism without seeking a visible reunion under the Successor of Peter. In 1938, he corresponded with Mother Maria Pia, Abbess of the Monastery of Grottaferrata in Italy, and he told her of Catholics, Protestants and Orthodox Christians who offered their lives for the unity of the Church. Mother Maria Gabriella, a young nun at the monastery, was inspired by the Holy Spirit to offer her life also, and she died on April 23, 1939, on Good Shepherd Sunday. Pope John Paul II beatified her as Maria Gabriella of Unity on January 25, 1983, the last day of the week of Prayer for Christian Unity. She had dedicated her life to the Priestly Prayer of Christ in John, chapter 17.

In summary, the Holy Spirit leads peoples and nations on myriad paths toward the salvation of mankind and the unity of the Church. This continuous and invisible work is evident, as it were, in two converging paths towards religious truth and practice: conversions to the Catholic Church and the ecumenical movement. Today John Henry Newman continues to guide men and women to the fullness of the Catholic faith, especially through his *Essay on Development*. But his arguments on the notes of the Church, the office of the pope, and the role of the Virgin Mary in salvation history, as well as his example of charity toward Christians of different ecclesial bodies, can also shed light on the vital work of ecumenism.

Sixteen

NEWMAN'S DEVOTION TO THE MOTHER OF GOD

A correct understanding of the Marian doctrine and the acceptance of a sound devotion to Mary are among the major difficulties encountered by converts to the Roman Catholic faith. This was not exactly the case with Newman although certain expressions of popular devotion to Mary did present a difficulty for him. Newman's relationship with Mary, the Mother of God, evolved through a series of phases from his early youth to adulthood. From his earlier consideration of Mary as an object of idolatry on the part of Roman Catholics, he went on to grasp a doctrinal belief in her role in salvation history; and later, while maintaining this belief, adopted a filial attitude towards her.

A strange and no less beautiful foreshadowing of Newman's devotion took place when he was not quite yet ten. As an adult he recounted the discovery of an old school copy book in which on the first page he had written, "John H. Newman, February 11th, 1811, Verse Book." Between the words "verse" and "book" he had drawn a solid cross and some beads that looked like a necklace.[1] He could only imagine that he had gotten the idea from a story or a religious picture and commented:

> But the strange thing is, how, among the thousand objects which meet a boy's eyes, these in particular should so have fixed themselves in my mind, that I made them thus practically my own. I am certain there was nothing in the churches I attended, or the prayer books that I read, to suggest them.[2]

[1] See *Apo.*, 107.
[2] *Apo.*, 107.

In his upbringing in a Low Church Anglican family and school, Newman was not exposed to the devotion to saints. On the contrary, some readings that he encountered at his boarding school presented Catholic practices as idolatrous. However, once he was at Oriel College, through the influence of his friend, Richard Hurrell Froude, he began to discover the lives of saints, the doctrine of the Holy Eucharist, and the Prayer of the Divine Office.

Gradually Newman began to put aside Calvinist and Evangelical beliefs. Through his reading of the Scriptures and of the church fathers, he acquired a doctrinal appreciation of Mary as the New Eve who untied the knot tied by the First Eve—a doctrine first espoused by St. Irenaeus of Lyons. If the First Adam was followed by Jesus (the New Adam), then Eve, too, was followed by Mary (the New Eve).

He still had objections to other Catholic beliefs and practices but considered these with less bias and more calm. Living at Oxford, he had before his very eyes evident signs of an earlier devotion to Mary. He beheld, for example, in the courtyard of Oriel College, over an archway, a small statue of the Virgin Mary; and the university church, of which he would become rector, was named after St. Mary, the Virgin.

Nonetheless, during the years before becoming Roman Catholic, Newman had difficulty in fully understanding the Church's belief and veneration of the Virgin Mary. Newman scholar Bishop Phillip Boyce has identified four periods in Newman's gradual development in devotion to the Virgin.[3] During a first period until 1834, the central role of Mary in the mystery of the Incarnation led him to doctrinal veneration of the Virgin Mother.

In a second period until 1837, Newman accepted the difference between intercession and invocation of Mary and the saints. This was a distinction tacitly recognized by the Articles: intercession was allowed, whereas invocation was condemned. At first Newman thought that invocation of the saints was not practiced in early Christianity. He thought that it obscured the unique media-

---

[3] John Henry Newman, *Mary: The Virgin Mary in the Life and Writings of John Henry Newman*, ed. Philip Boyce (Grand Rapids: Eerdmans Publishing Co, 2001), 27-32.

tion of Christ and that it could lead to idolatry. When he and his companions at Littlemore prayed the Divine Office, they refrained from praying *ora pro nobis* (pray for us) and, instead, prayed *oret pro nobis* (may she intercede for us), and they omitted the ancient hymn *Salve Regina.*

Out of obedience to the Anglican Church, Newman followed Anglican practices until his reception into the Roman Church. While still an Anglican he told Mary Holmes, one of the women to whom he gave spiritual direction, not to invoke the saints. He thought it was correct to ask God to allow Mary to pray for one's intentions but that one should not pray directly to the Virgin Mary.[4] Newman gave the same advice to others, saying to them that they should avoid mixing what he called two "systems" of worship.

In a third period from 1837 to 1839, he condemned as unscriptural the external veneration of Mary by modern Catholics, yet all the while his own veneration for her continued to grow. In a last period from 1839 to 1845, as Newman's understanding of true doctrinal development and practices grew, he finally understood and accepted the modern Catholic veneration of the Virgin Mary.

Newman dedicated the last pages of his *Essay on Development* to the development of Christian belief and devotion to the saints, in particular to the Blessed Virgin Mary. He explained how the church fathers before the Council of Nicea spoke in the second and third centuries of the Virgin Mary as the New Eve and gave her singular honor as the Mother of the New Adam. He asserted that devotion to the Mother of God was an illustration of the sixth note of true development of doctrine—the conservative action of development on an earlier doctrine. For him devotion to the Mother of God provided protection and confirmation of the divinity of her Son.[5] From a doctrinal point of view, it did so by underlining Christ's divinity and sinlessness, as in the case of the dogma of Mary's Immaculate Conception.

---

[4] See JHN to Mary Holmes (June 10, 1844), *LD*, Vol. 10: 267.
[5] *Dev.*, 425-436.

By mid-1845, Newman no longer had any intellectual doubts about Roman Catholic doctrine; yet, while he labored over the *Essay on Development*, his family and friends continued to give him unsolicited suggestions and advice against his intended step to embrace Catholicism. On August 22, 1845, Newman entered the word "medal" in his diary: it marked the day that he began to wear around his neck the Miraculous Medal, a gift from George Tickell, a recent convert from Anglicanism.[6]

Newman's devotion to the Virgin Mary was rooted in doctrinal piety, which is evident in the short texts that he wrote for each of the days of the month of May, traditionally dedicated in the Church to Marian devotion. Almost at the very start of these meditations, on May 3, he would focus on the doctrine of Mary's Immaculate Conception:

> He who was born from Eternity was born by an eternal decree to save us in Time, and to redeem the whole race; and Mary's redemption was determined in that special manner which we call the Immaculate Conception. It was decreed, not that she should be *cleansed* from sin, but that she should, from the first moment of her being, be *preserved* from sin; so that the Evil One never had any part in her. Therefore, she was a child of Adam and Eve as if they had never fallen; she did not share with them their sin; she inherited the gifts and graces (and more than those) which Adam and Eve possessed in Paradise. This is her prerogative, and the foundation of all those salutary truths which are revealed to us concerning her. Let us say then with all holy souls, *Virgin most pure, conceived without original sin, Mary, pray for us.*[7]

For a meditation a few days later in May, Newman chose one of the titles of Mary, *virgo praedicanda* (the one who should be preached). He noted that devotion to her has grown gradually with successive ages:

---

[6] In an apparition in Paris in 1830, the Virgin Mary instructed St. Catherine Labouré to have made a medal in honor of her Immaculate Conception and promised great graces to those who wore it.

[7] *MD*, 9.

Not so much preached about her in early times as in later. First she was preached as the Virgin of Virgins—then as the Mother of God—then as glorious in her Assumption—then as the Advocate of sinners—then as Immaculate in her Conception. And this last has been the special preaching of the present century; and thus that which was earliest in her own history is the latest in the Church's recognition of her.[8]

Newman offered other beautiful explanations for the titles given to Mary in the Litany of Loreto. For instance, for the title *domus aurea* (House of Gold) he writes:

She is the house and the palace of the Great King, of God Himself. Our Lord, the Co-equal Son of God, once dwelt in her. He was her Guest; nay, more than a guest, for a guest comes into a house as well as leaves it. But our Lord was actually *born in* this holy house. He took His flesh and His blood from this house, from the flesh, from the veins of Mary. Rightly then was she made to be of pure gold, because she was to give of that gold to form the body of the Son of God. She was *golden* in her conception, *golden* in her birth. She went through the fire of her suffering like gold in the furnace, and when she ascended on high, she was, in the words of our hymn: Above all the Angels in glory untold, Standing next to the King in a vesture of gold.[9]

Although this English priest appreciated poetic imagery and verse, he did not like the Italian sentimentality of the Catholic devotional books that he had been given. Having lived in Rome, he had firsthand experience of Italy and objected to imposing an Italian character on English devotion—which is what Faber and the other Oratorians in London wished to do. Despite the marked difference with the "style" of St. Alphonse Liguori or the French St. Louis Marie de Montfort, his references and prayers to Mary showed an affectionate love for her. This is especially noticeable in

[8] *MD*, 12.
[9] *MD*, 16.

his meditations for the Stations of the Cross, composed in 1860.

The Virgin Mary appears throughout Newman's consideration of the Passion. He referred repeatedly to her profound suffering, and her mediation on behalf of her Son. He envisioned that Mary sent Simon of Cyrene and Veronica to help Jesus.

In the Fourth Station on Jesus' encounter with his mother, Newman gave an outline of Mary's life intimately tied to the life of her Son:

> THERE is no part of the history of Jesus, but Mary has her part in it. There are those who profess to be His servants, who think that her work was ended when she bore Him and after that she had nothing to do, but disappear and be forgotten. But we, O Lord, Thy children of the Catholic Church, do not so think of Thy Mother. She brought the tender infant into the Temple, she lifted Him up in her arms when the wise men came to adore Him. She fled with Him to Egypt, she took Him up to Jerusalem when He was twelve years old. He lived with her at Nazareth for thirty years. She was with Him at the marriage-feast. Even when He had left her to preach, she hovered about Him. And now she shows herself as He toils along the Sacred Way with His cross on His shoulders.[10]

Newman closes this short reflection with a tender invocation to Mary that shows the spiritual dimension of his devotion to her: "Sweet Mother, let us ever think of thee when we think of Jesus, and when we pray to Him, ever aid us by thy powerful intercession." She was for him, as she is for all Christians, a mother.

In the next to last station, he offers some words of condolence and consolation to our Blessed Mother:

> He has not been in Thy arms, O Mother of God, since He was a child—but now thou hast a claim upon Him, when the world has done its worst. For thou art the all-favoured, all-blessed, all-gracious Mother of the Highest. We rejoice in this great mystery. He has been hidden in thy womb, He has lain

10 *MD*, 158.

in thy bosom, He has been suckled at thy breasts, He has been carried in thy arms—and now that He is dead, He is placed upon thy lap. Virgin Mother of God, pray for us.[11]

Newman thus combined doctrine with devotion. Mary, the Virgin of Nazareth, who is full of grace and who became the mother of the Savior, was given to us to be our mother. Yet he always pointed to the doctrinal foundations for religious practices, as he did in an open letter to Edward Pusey. In 1865, his old friend Pusey had published a book titled *Eirenicon* to counter Roman Catholic practices and dissuade Anglicans from becoming Roman Catholics. The book, which was in response to another by Manning, took special aim at doctrine and devotion concerning the Virgin Mary and papal infallibility. Although in it Pusey quoted and criticized the extreme positions of ultramontane Catholics such as Faber, Manning, and W.G. Ward,[12] Newman told Pusey that it was a "rhetorical and unfair"[13] book that, instead of smoothing contrarieties, aggravated them and would in all likelihood justly anger Catholics.[14] Friends asked Newman to rebut this book, setting forth a clear and moderate understanding of Catholic beliefs and practices; as well as removing Anglican fears aroused by so-called Catholic beliefs that were put forth by the *Dublin Review*, a publication that acted as the self-appointed official interpreter of Catholic truths.

In his public reply to Pusey, in which Newman limited himself to doctrine and devotion to Mary, he asked for the foundation of this devotion:

What is the great rudimental teaching of Antiquity from its earliest date concerning her? By "rudimental teaching," I

---

[11] *MD*, 167.

[12] Newman published his reply as a book titled *A Letter to the Rev. E. B. Pusey, D.D. on his recent Eirenicon*. It was published in January 1866, and two thousand copies were sold in a fortnight.

[13] JHN to Edward B. Pusey, (October 31, 1866), *LD*, Vol. 22: 89. Pusey was in fact exploring a possible corporate reunion between Anglicans and Catholics, and had then just met with the Archbishop of Paris, Georges Darboy, on this very subject.

[14] See JHN to Mrs. William Froude, (October 16, 1866), *LD*, Vol. 22: 76; also see Ker's *John Henry Newman*, 578-579.

mean the *primâ facie* view of her person and office, the broad
outline laid down of her, the aspect under which she comes to
us, in the writings of the Fathers. She is the Second Eve.[15]

Newman distinguished between what the Church believes and
teaches and what a person is capable of understanding—an individual who does not need to understand every truth to be saved or
to accept every detail of devotion. He wrote a private letter to
Pusey stating he had never heard of Louis Marie de Montfort, and
did not have a text attributed to the Spanish theologian Francisco
Suarez: 'No one is saved who is not *devout* to Mary'. Newman
argued that one did not need to have devotion to Mary to be
saved, "(B)ut it may be quite true nevertheless, that Mary's *intercession* is a necessary part of the economy of redemption, just as
Eve co-operated in Adam's fall."[16]

In a homily, *Mary's Glory for the Sake of her Son*, Newman points
out that all the dogmas about the Virgin Mary serve to teach us
about the divinity of Christ, and to foster and protect doctrine
concerning Jesus. This argument, unknown to many in his time,
continues to be unknown for some today who think that Mary is
a distraction from biblical teaching and the true worship of Christ.
Instead, Newman drew from biblical passages and texts from the
church fathers to elucidate the various Marian dogmas such as
Mary's Assumption into heaven.

Love for Mary, the Mother of God, was manifest in many ways
in Newman's life. Besides his writings on and prayers to her, he
named the university church in Dublin with one of the titles traditionally given to Mary: *Sedes Sapientiae* (Seat of Wisdom). Giv-
en the nature of the university, the title of its church was particularly appropriate.

At the Oratory School he organized with Fr. Ambrose St. John,
Marian devotions took place during the month of May. Throughout the year the boys were also invited to pray the Rosary. From

---

[15] *A Letter to the Rev. E. B. Pusey, D.D. on his recent Eirenicon, in Diff.*, Vol. 2: 31.
[16] JHN to Edward B. Pusey, (October 31, 1866), LD, Vol. 22: 90.

what Newman preached to the boys at the nearby Oscott College on the feast of Our Lady of the Holy Rosary, October 5, 1879, we have his thoughts on this cherished Catholic practice. He said of the Rosary: "It seems so simple and easy, but you know God chooses the small things of the world to humble the great."[17]

Next he explained to the boys that the great power of the Rosary lies in the belief that it brings the truths of the Creed closer home to us:

> . . . of course, the Creed is in some sense a prayer and a great act of homage to God; but the Rosary gives us the great truths of His life and death to meditate upon, and brings them nearer to our hearts.[18]

Lastly he invited the boys to consider the Holy Family, including St. Joseph, and their own families, which they would one day leave to go out into the world. They would only then fully appreciate the need to be close to the Holy Family:

> You look forward to the time when you will go out into the world, and it seems to you very bright and full of promise. It is not wrong for you to look forward to that time; but most men who know the world find it a world of great trouble, and disappointments, and even misery. If it turns out so to you, seek a home in the Holy Family that you think about in the mysteries of the Rosary.[19]

In summary, Blessed Newman overcame early childhood Protestant biases against Catholic beliefs and reached a mature doctrinal belief in the Virgin Mary's gifts and role in salvation history. Together with this, he developed a devotion to her which was both personal and tender—that of a son to a mother. His consider-

---

[17] John Henry Newman, "To Boys, about the Rosary," [Oscott College, October 5, 1879] in *Sayings of Cardinal Newman*, ed. anonymous (London: Burns & Oates, Ltd.), available at www.newmanreader.org.

[18] *Sayings of Cardinal Newman*, 44.

[19] *Sayings of Cardinal Newman*, 45.

ations and sermons on Mary, the Mother of God, are a rich source of inspiration for those who read them. While the tone of his expressions differs from those of a St. Alfonse Liguori or a St. Louis Marie de Montfort, he fully agreed with their doctrine and in substance with their devotion.

Holiness in a Secular Age: The Witness of Cardinal Newman

Each saint, regardless of the time in which he lives, sheds light and peace around him, making God present to the world. The chapters of this book have been an attempt to show the way that John Henry Newman did this in his own time and continues to do so in ours. He stands as a credible witness to holiness in a secular age. This is due in large part because of similarities between the nineteenth century to our century, namely, its rationalism and materialism as well as growing agnosticism and atheism. Newman addressed these serious ills of society, recognizing with great acuity the roots of the problems and offering the solutions provided by reason and revelation.

At the beatification of Cardinal Newman, Pope Benedict XVI referred to Newman's distinction as a priest, placing him together with venerable English saints:

> England has a long tradition of martyr saints, whose courageous witness has sustained and inspired the Catholic community here for centuries. Yet it is right and fitting that we should recognize today the holiness of a confessor, a son of this nation who, while not called to shed his blood for the Lord, nevertheless bore eloquent witness to him in the course of a long life devoted to the priestly ministry, and especially to preaching, teaching, and writing. He is worthy to take his place in a long line of saints and scholars from these islands, Saint Bede, Saint Hilda, Saint Aelred, Blessed Duns Scotus, to name but a few.[1]

---

[1] Benedict XVI, Papal Homily at the Beatification of Cardinal Newman, Birmingham, England, September 19, 2010. www.zenit.org/article-30411?I=english

In particular, the pope highlighted his scholarship, wisdom and love for God, manifested in his holy life:

> In Blessed John Henry, that tradition of gentle scholarship, deep human wisdom and profound love for the Lord has borne rich fruit, as a sign of the abiding presence of the Holy Spirit deep within the heart of God's people, bringing forth abundant gifts of holiness.[2]

These qualities are ones desired for all Christians but which were lived in exemplary manner by the saints. In a time in Western culture, marked by materialism, hedonism, relativism and skepticism, there is great need for holy men and women, moved by the Holy Spirit, striving to gain wisdom and live lives of charity.

In Blessed Newman we find the best of classical scholarship necessary to combat the relativism and consequent skepticism that pervade so much of social life and educational institutions. Newman thought the work of defending moral truths and the Church's teachings required a good education of the laity. His vision and actual work at the Catholic University of Ireland is beginning to inspire the work of some colleges and institutes of Catholic studies.

Newman argued that university students should develop their intellects by acquiring a philosophical habit of mind—here lies the challenge for today's students and educators. At the same time these young men and women must develop their character through religious instruction and spiritual advice. The goal of a university with regard to its students is to 'make them men' or 'women' as the case may be. Learning more about Cardinal Newman's life and proposing his writings to students at Newman Centers in universities throughout North America and similar institutions in other English speaking countries would contribute to a revival of Catholic education.

The real purpose of a university education is the development and growth of the intellect and moral character of students; it is

---

[2] *Ibid.*

not, as is extolled today, to acquire a profession or trade—there are graduate schools and trade schools for that—and, even less to acquire a smattering of general knowledge and a superficial tolerance of every belief. The latter is the incomplete 'idea of a gentleman,' often mistakenly attributed to Newman's authorship.

It bears repeating that the long description of the gentleman that Newman gives in *The Idea of a University* is far from his view. That is a purely natural look at the human being, ignoring his weaknesses and sinfulness, and his need for redemption and grace. Although the world holds up for us the ideal of a gentleman with many human talents and interests, the true believer aspires to a higher ideal: that of a Christian gentleman or lady, a man or woman, who lives the supernatural life of a child of God.

As much as Newman realized the importance of a good university education he thought the work of education must begin with teaching boys and helping their parents to complement the work done at school. Neither the state nor a school can substitute, much less supplant, parents in their role as the primary educators. His work with parents at the Oratory School is an invitation for teachers and parents to work more closely in the education of children.

Newman's convincing explanation of the harmony between faith and reason can be of great benefit to contemporary students of the sciences who are told by others that faith is opposed to science or is at least a hindrance. At the Catholic University of Ireland he taught students to think about the correct relationship between the two, and established the school of medicine and the school of sciences based on this very notion.

With the aid of faith and reason the layperson has to know and practice his faith well. If he does not he will be gradually swallowed up by the concerns of the world, and then by worldliness. The Church needs, and God wishes, that his children act as a leaven in society to spread God's reign of peace and love in the world, preparing men for the fulfillment of the kingdom in heaven.

The loss or weakening of faith in our times is directly related to the increasing materialism and hedonism of Western civilization with its secularist denial of the soul. Newman challenges Christians to overcome these strangleholds by opening their minds to spiritual and intellectual reality. Through daily prayer and growth in the virtues, and a frequent encounter with Christ in the sacraments the Christian advances in holiness.

Newman advocated the pursuit of this holiness by all men and women, not only by priests and members of religious orders. As before him St. Philip Neri, St. Francis de Sales, Blessed Frederic Ozanam, and after him St. Josemaría, Blessed Alvaro del Portillo and St. John Paul II, he presented the laity with a real path and example to holiness within their reach in all walks of life.

In the words of Pope Benedict, Newman understood the human desire for an intimate communion with God:

> Cardinal Newman's motto, *Cor ad cor loquitur*, or "Heart speaks unto heart", gives us an insight into his understanding of the Christian life as a call to holiness, experienced as the profound desire of the human heart to enter into intimate communion with the Heart of God. He reminds us that faithfulness to prayer gradually transforms us into the divine likeness. As he wrote in one of his many fine sermons, "a habit of prayer, the practice of turning to God and the unseen world in every season, in every place, in every emergency— prayer, I say, has what may be called a natural effect in spiritualizing and elevating the soul. A man is no longer what he was before; gradually . . . he has imbibed a new set of ideas, and become imbued with fresh principles" (Parochial and Plain Sermons, iv, 230-231).[3]

At a time when many people seek God purely through contact with nature and in an individual manner, ignoring or forgetting the supernatural communication of the divine through grace, and the mediation of the Church, Newman's meditation of the Scrip-

---

[3] *Ibid.*

tures can teach people a great deal. Newman went to the Scriptures as a preeminent place of encounter with God. He saw the need for the aid of languages and history to understand the literal meaning of the Scriptures, but warned against excesses in historical and literary analyses of the Scriptures that empty the Word of God of its power and mystery. For this reason he privileged the spiritual understanding of the Scriptures. For him the Bible must foremost be understood as the Word of God, which comes to man through the Church, and which must be interpreted in the context of the Church's living Tradition and authority.

For Newman, however, the living Word of God is conveyed in a very special way through the mysteries or sacraments of the Church, and not only through sermons—which he correctly identified was the focus of Protestant and Anglican services. God reveals himself through the sacramental signs in the liturgy, and in this setting the Word of God is preached as a part of the whole.

At the very heart of God's revelation and teaching on holiness is the virtue of charity, which Pope Benedict indicated that Newman lived so well it was recognized by his non-Catholic neighbors in the city of Birmingham. The source of this service to men practiced by Newman and his fellow Oratorians was friendship with God. And Newman's example and sermons move us to live charity better with those who are in need of assistance such as the sick, unemployed and immigrants.

Naturally Newman lived charity with his numerous friends. He was their good and loyal friend. His friendships were characterized by sincerity, mutual respect and warmth. Often when friends moved, the friendships were maintained through regular correspondence and mutual prayer. We are reminded through his life's example that it is usually through friendship that the kingdom of God grows.

Whereas all saints have by the very definition of sainthood lived the virtues of faith, hope and charity to the highest degree, Newman, like other modern saints such as St. Josemaría Escrivá and John Paul II, also excelled in intellectual talents, which he placed at the service of God in the Church. He was a prolific writer and apologist and his works can easily reach a large population of the world today because he spoke the English language.

Each of the chapters of this book points to Newman's rich contributions to the Church and his witness of holiness in society but if we were to choose those that speak most to the spirit of our secular age we would indicate those that present his teaching on the moral conscience, religious truth and doctrinal development. Newman addressed the problem of relativism, which he called "liberalism in religion" his entire life and gave us a way of understanding objective truths in doctrine. In a similar way he helps us to see the necessary connection between objective truth and our moral choices in life. In other words, doctrinal and moral truths are not arbitrary, or subject to preferences or opinion. They enable us to know reality as it really is, and to seek what is true, good and beautiful; and ultimately to achieve our final happiness with God.

Following the tradition of the Church Newman taught that reason illumined by faith, and guided by the teaching of the Church allows men to distinguish truth from error, both in doctrine and in morals. Put even more clearly, the moral conscience does not create the truth. Furthermore, in a society that rationalizes behavior contrary to the natural law and the worship of God, even more so than in Newman's own age, he presents us with the challenge of convincing others of the truth, through our friendship and example, and always speaking the truth in charity (*veritates facientem in caritate*).[4]

---

[4] Letter to the Ephesians 4:15.

Bibliography

Balaguer, Vincente. "La Constitución Dogmática *Dei Verbum*" in *Annuarium Historiae Conciliorum* 43 (2011), 31-71.

Barbeau, Jeffrey. W. "Newman and the Interpretation of Inspired Scripture," *Theological Studies* 63 (2002), 62. Website: http://cdn.theologicalstudies.net/63/63.1/63.1.3.pdf.

Benedict XVI. Papal Homily at the Mass with the Beatification of Venerable Cardinal John Henry Newman in Birmingham, England (September 19, 2010). Vatican website: www.vatican.va.

Blehl, Vincent Ferrer, S. J. *The White Stone: The Spiritual Theology of John Henry Newman*. Petersham, Mass.: St. Bede's Publications, 1993.

Bouyer, Louis. *Newman: His Life and Spirituality: An Intellectual and Spiritual Biography of John Henry Newman*. Translated by J. Lewis May. San Francisco: Ignatius Press, 2011.

Brown, Peter. *Augustine of Hippo, a Biography*. Berkeley: University of California Press, 2000.

Cicero. *Laelius de Amicitia*. 6. Website: http://penelope.uchicago.edu/Thayer/E/Roman/Texts/Cicero/Laelius_de_Amicitia/text*.html.

de Sales, Frances, and Jane de Chantal. *Francis de Sales, Jane de Chantal: Letters of Spiritual Direction*. Edited by Péronne Marie Thibert, V. H. M., Wendy M. Wright, and Joseph Power, O. S. F. S. Mahwah, N.J.: Paulist Press, 1988.

Dessain, Charles Stephen. *John Henry Newman*. Oxford: Oxford University Press, 1980.

Dulles, Avery. *John Henry Newman*, London: Continuum, 2002.

Friedel, Francis J. *The Mariology of Cardinal Newman*. New York: Benzinger Brothers, 1928.

Guardini, Romano. *The Living God*. New York: Pantheon Books, 1957.

Holmes, J. Derek. "Newman's Attitude towards Historical Criticism and Biblical Inspiration," *Downside Review* 89 (1971): 22-37.

Honoré, Jean. *The Spiritual Journey of Newman.* New York: Alba House, 1992.

Hulsman, John. *The Rule of Our Warfare: John Henry Newman and the True Christian Life.* New York: Scepter Publishers, 2003.

Jaki, Stanley. *Newman to Converts: An Existential Ecclesiology.* Pinckney, Mich.: Real View Books, 2001.

John Paul II. Encyclical Letter *Fides et ratio* (September 14, 1998), n. 74. Vatican website : www.vatican.va.

John Paul II, Encyclical letter *Ut Unum Sint* (May 25, 1995), n. 36. Vatican website: www.vatican.va.

John Paul II. Letter on the Occasion of the Centenary of the Cardinalate of J. H. Newman. April 7, 1979. *Newman Reader.* The National Institute for Newman Studies website: http://www.newmanreader.org/canonization/popes/or21may79.html.

John Paul II, Letter on the Occasion of the 2nd Centenary of the Birth of Cardinal John Henry Newman. January 22, 2001. Vatican website: http://w2.vatican.va/content/john-paul-ii/en/letters/2001/documents/hf_jp-ii_let_20010227_john-henry-newman.html.

Jullian, Paula M.. ed. *La Idea de Una Universidad,* Chile: Ediciones Universidad Católica de Chile, 2016.

Ker, Ian. *John Henry Newman,* Oxford: Oxford University Press, 1988.

Ker, Ian. *Newman on Vatican II,* Oxford: Oxford University Press, 2014.

Ligouri, Alphonse. *Theologia Moralis,* Part 1, Chapter 1. Website: https://archive.org/stream/theologiamorali04mansgoog#page/n84/mode/2up

Martin, Brian. *John Henry Newman, His Life and Work.* London: Continuum, 2000.

Meszaros, Andrew. '*Haec Traditio proficit*': Congar's Reception of Newman in Dei Verbum, Section 8. New Black Friars, 92 (2011): 247-254.

Morales Marín, José. *John Henry Newman (1801-1890)*. Madrid: Ediciones Rialp, 1990.

Morgan, Drew. "John Henry Newman—Doctor of Conscience: Doctor of the Church?" *Newman Studies Journal*, 4: no. 1 (Spring 2007): 5-23.

Newman, John Henry. Various works. Unless otherwise noted are usually taken from the uniform edition of 1868-1881 (36 volumes) published by Longmans, Green and Co., London. The texts can be consulted online at the Newman Reader website: www.newmanreader.org

———*Letter and Diaries of John Henry Newman*, ed. Charles Stephen Dessain et al (Oxford and London: 1961-). The texts can be consulted online at the Newman Reader website: www.newmanreader.org

———*Mary: The Virgin Mary in the Life and Writings of John Henry Newman.* Edited by Philip Boyce. Grand Rapids: Eerdmans Publishing Co, 2001.

———*Meditations and Devotions of the Late Cardinal Newman.* Edited by William Neville. London: Longmans, Green, and Co, 1907.

———*My Campaign in Ireland, Part I: Catholic University Reports and Other Papers.* Aberdeen: A. King, 1896.

———*On the Inspiration of Scripture.* Edited by J. Derek Holmes and Robert Murray. Holmes, Washington, D.C.: Corpus Books, 1967.

Paul VI, Dogmatic Constitution on Divine Revelation *Dei Verbum.* November 18, 1965. Vatican website: www.vatican.va.

Second Vatican' Council. Decree on Ecumenism *Unitatis Redintegratio* (November 21, 1964), n. 8. Vatican website: www.vatican.va.

Short, Edward. *Newman and his Contemporaries.* New York: T & T Clark, 2011.

Shrimpton, Paul. *A Catholic Eton? Newman's Oratory School.* Leominster, UK: Gracewing, 2005.

Shrimpton, Paul. *The 'Making of Men,' The Idea and reality of*

Newman's university in Oxford and Dublin. Leominster, UK: Gracewing, 2014.

Trevor, Meriol. Newman: *The Pillar of the Cloud* and *Light in Winter.* London: Macmillan & Co., Ltd, 1962.

Rupert, Jane. *John Henry Newman on the Nature of the Mind: Reason in Religion, Science, and the Humanities.* New York: Lexington Books, 2011.

Various authors, *Newman Studies Journal,* 2004-2017.

Vélez, Juan R. *Passion for Truth: The Life of John Henry Newman.* Charlotte: TAN Books, 2012.

Vorgrimler, Herbert, General Ed. *Commentary of the Documents of Vatican II,* Vol. III. Burns & Oates, Herder and Herder, 1969.

Index

Photo Credits

1. Newman family sketch by Maria Giberne. Courtesy of International Centre of Newman Friends.

2. Trinity College, Oxford. Courtesy of Olivia Kirwan.

3. Quad at Oriel College, Oxford. Courtesy of Paul Shrimpton.

4. University Church of St. Mary the Virgin, Oxford. Courtesy of Olivia Kirwan.

5. The pulpit of St. Mary the Virgin. Courtesy of International Centre of Newman Friends.

6. Church of St. Mary and St. Nicholas in Littlemore. Courtesy of International Centre of Newman Friends.

7. Engraving of Newman by Henry Maclean. Courtesy of International Centre of Newman Friends.

8. Newman's desk at Littlemore. Courtesy of International Centre of Newman Friends.

9. University House. 87 St. Stephen's Green, Dublin. Courtesy of Guillermo Dillon.

10. Interior of the University Church Our Lady Seat of Wisdom, Dublin. Courtesy of Bruce Wyman.

11. Newman's writing desk in his room at the Birmingham Oratory. Courtesy of the Fathers of the Birmingham Oratory.

12. Fr. Newman, ca 1866. Courtesy of International Centre of Newman Friends.

13. Photograph of Cardinal Newman by Louis Barraud. (1885). Courtesy of the Fathers of the Birmingham Oratory.

14. Cardinal Newman Library at the Birmingham Oratory. Courtesy of the Fathers of the Birmingham Oratory.

15. Cardinal Newman's private Chapel at the Birmingham Oratory. Courtesy of the Fathers of the Birmingham Oratory.

16. Newman's tombstone at Rednal, outside Birmingham. Courtesy of the Fathers of the Birmingham Oratory.